COLORADO MOUNTAIN SKI TOURS AND HIKES

A Year Round Guide

Dave Muller

Library of Congress Catalog Card No. 93-83727

Muller, Dave
**COLORADO MOUNTAIN SKI TOURS AND HIKES:
A Year Round Guide**

ISBN: 0-9619666-1-0

First Edition
1 2 3 4 5 6 7 8 9

Printed in the United States of America

Front cover photo: *Navajo Peak from Pawnee Pass Trail.*

Back cover photos: *Rabbit Ears Peak and Lake Dillon from Ptarmigan Peak.*

All photographs by the author

CONTENTS

CONTENTS (continued)

CONTENTS (continued)

ACKNOWLEDGEMENTS

I thank the many persons who helped in the realization of this guide book. My wife, Jackie, accompanied me on many of these outings and has been a great source of support and inspiration. Mairi Hamilton Clark typed, coordinated and encouraged throughout the preparation. My parents, Irish-American, Margaret and Swiss, Albert made it all possible and my son, Paul, showed me the way. Chuck Hohnstein and the good people of Quality Press put everything in its final form.

My companions on these outings include Tony, June, Lauren and Anthony Bianchi, John and Mellie Brand, Mary, Claire and Adam Brewer, S. Macon and Ginny Cowles, Marty and Bonnie Curtan, Ina Mae Denham, Nick DiBella, Bob and Geri Eddy, Anita and Ron Farenbach, Barbara Fenton, Kit Hevron, Karen Jones, Chuck Johnson, Kent and Liz Kreider, Jim Mahoney, Andrew, Taree and Katie Muller, Matthew, Sara and Tom Muller, Don O'Brien, Chris Ruskey, Sam Seymour, Patrick and Shannon Walsh, Jonathan Walter and Art Warner.

I thank the U.S. Geologic Survey, Jefferson County Open Space, the National Forest Service, the cities of Lakewood and Boulder, and Trails Illustrated for permission to reproduce parts of their maps.

The staff of the Denver Post has been most helpful in their weekly presentation of many of these outings and in their permission to use that material. And my greatest appreciation goes to the Creator of the universe who has given so lavishly to Colorado.

SKI TOUR DESTINATIONS

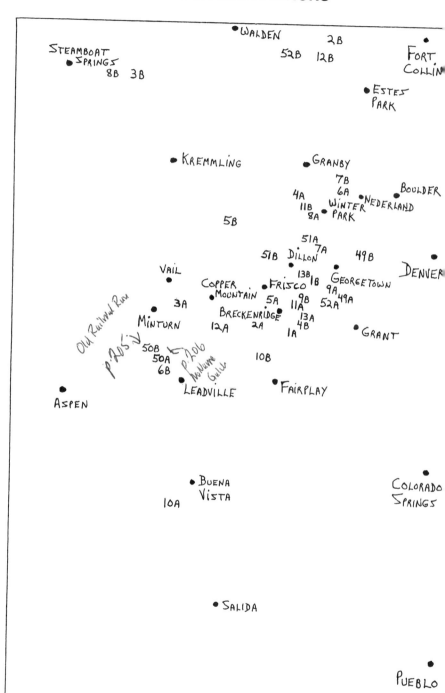

HIKE DESTINATIONS

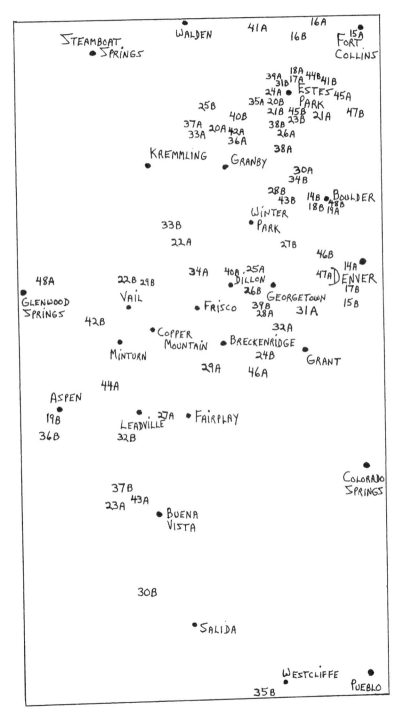

INTRODUCTION

Two themes direct this book. The first is that the Colorado Mountains are for everyone's enjoyment. The second is that an outdoor guide should provide enough data so that one doesn't get lost, or ruin a day in the mountains in confusion and frustration. In more than twenty-two years as a Colorado resident, I continue to be awed by the beauty and the peace of our public lands and therefore want to promote their enjoyment.

After writing *Colorado Mountain Hikes for Everyone*, I began a weekly "Hike of the Week" column on the sports pages of *The Denver Post*. This led to the "Ski Tour of the Week" for the four coldest months (December through March). As this column has continued for over four years, the material for a year around hiking and cross country skiing guide emerged. Hiking and ski touring are not too different. Neither requires great athletic ability or lessons and the individual is not forced into crowded settings (as in downhill skiing).

This guide book describes two outings for each of the 52 weeks of the year. The first thirteen weeks are devoted to ski touring. Weeks fourteen through forty-eight are for hiking, and weeks forty-nine through fifty-two are for December cross country skiing. The author has made all of these hikes and ski tours himself. Barring unusual weather conditions, the hike and tour numbers correspond to the time of year in which they can be done. Of course, a November hike can be done in August but not necessarily vice-versa.

HIKE OR SKI TOUR SPECIFICATIONS:

The two major facts in judging the difficulty of an outing are the distance and the elevation gain. Distances given are for one way to the destination unless a loop is described. The times are the author's and are provided as a point of reference and not a standard. (I'm a more proficient hiker than cross country skier.) The elevation gain will include the extra footage required when there are undulations in the trail.

AVALANCHE DANGER:

For each ski tour I provide three levels of rating: least, moderate and significant. Weather conditions, such as recent snowfall, can change a specific rating. The reader is urged to become knowledgeable about avalanche dangers.

DIFFICULTY:

There are three levels of difficulty for ski touring: easiest, more difficult and most difficult. These conform to the green, blue and black signs seen along some ski touring routes. For hiking, four levels of difficulty are listed: easy, moderate, more difficult and most difficult. Adverse weather conditions can increase the difficulty of any hike or ski tour.

The ski tours and hikes are listed by their level of difficulty in Tables I and II. The easiest will be listed first and the level of difficulty increases as one goes down the list.

STEEPNESS INDEX:

Since elevation gain is such a key factor in the difficulty of a mountain hike or ski tour, I have listed the steepness index with each outing. This number is obtained by dividing the one-way length of a hike or ski tour in feet into the elevation gain for the entire outing. The higher the number, the greater is the steepness.

TRAILS:

All of these ski tours and hikes have trails. Markers on trees will often be present to help with trail finding. These may be blazes, (distinctive cuts on a tree trunk), ribbons, diamond signs, cairns or trail emblems. If there is no trail, a compass and the 7½ minute map for the area are strongly recommended. If you lose a trail, it is best to backtrack and explore where you lost it.

MAPS:

Several maps are listed for each outing. The most detailed and best are usually the 7½ minute maps. Trails Illustrated maps are very comprehensive and weather resistant. The county maps are quite detailed and are often good enough. The National Forest maps have little detail but cover a wider area and are good for identifying adjacent peaks. These maps can be purchased at certain sporting goods stores. The 7½ minute maps and county maps can also be obtained from the Department of the Interior and the National Forest maps from the U.S. Forest Service (Department of Agriculture).

SUMMIT VIEWS:

Compass directions to adjacent peaks are provided for the summit hikes to enhance your awareness and appreciation. These will be from the summit where the magnetic fields can cause varying readings. Not all visible peaks will be listed. Weather conditions, of course, may sometimes prevent certain mountains from being seen. A compass helps greatly in peak identification.

ROCKY MOUNTAIN NATIONAL PARK:

There are several Rocky Mountain National Park outings described in this guide. These involve excellent, well-marked trails. Additional information and the park map may be obtained at the visitors' centers at park entrances or within the park. An entrance fee is required when you enter the park at its main entrances but not at the Wild Basin area. There are special rules within the park including the prohibition of pets and vehicles on the trails.

RECOMMENDED EQUIPMENT:

For these outings a compass, good footwear, a hat or cap, sunscreen, adequate water (at least 1½ quart per person per half day), and a backpack with food and protection from the cold and rain are strongly advised. A flashlight, map, matches, a whistle and a survival blanket add little weight and may be lifesaving in case of emergency.

For ski touring a sporting goods store can advise you about skis, boots and poles. Be especially prepared for cold and wetness. Hypothermia and avalanches are the major dangers of ski touring.

In addition to being adequately prepared with equipment, maps and information, the reader is urged to be especially careful and conservative in decision making. It is very easy to get lost or be quickly enveloped by dangerous weather conditions in the mountains. Be aware that even a short fall onto a rocky surface can be catastrophic. Never proceed further if there is any doubt you can return by the same route.

TABLE I
SKI TOURS IN ORDER OF DIFFICULTY

TABLE II
HIKES IN ORDER OF DIFFICULTY

1A   Pennsylvania Creek

Tour Distance: 4.0 miles each way
Tour Time: Up in 115 minutes. Down in 105 minutes.
Starting Elevation: 10,315 feet
Highest Elevation: 11,740 feet (3578 meters)
Elevation Gain: 1,525 feet (includes 50 extra feet each way)
Avalanche Danger: Moderate
Difficulty: More Difficult
Steepness Index: 0.07
Trail: All the way
Relevant Maps: Breckenridge 7½ minute
                    Boreas Pass 7½ minute
                    Trails Illustrated Number 109
                    Summit County Number Two
                    Arapaho National Forest (Dillon Ranger District)

Getting There: From the stop light at Ski Hill Road in Breckenridge, drive south on Colorado 9 for 4.1 miles and turn left onto the Blue River Road. Avoid three consecutive right forks and drive for 0.25 miles on the Blue River Road and turn right at a sign stating "The Royal." Keep right after 0.05 miles farther and right again in 0.2 more miles at a sign for "The Coronet." Go straight at a 4-way intersection in 0.3 more miles and keep left 0.1 mile later. Then follow the main road till it ends in 0.4 miles from the last fork and park. The total distance from Colorado 9 to the parking area is 1.3 miles. Some regular cars can drive this far. Without four-wheel drive you may need to park farther down the road.

Pennsylvania Creek makes a good ski tour to start the new year. There should be enough snow as you ascend a scenic valley. The first mile is quite steep before you reach a clearing on the right. Since the ascent proceeds eastward, be careful about protection from the sun.

Begin northwest from the parking area on a clear trail. The route soon turns right (east) ascending steeply before becoming more gradual in its middle segment. At 2.6 miles you will cross Pennsylvania Creek. Some may wish to stop at this point. After the creek the trail ascends more steeply and curves to the south. Keep right at two forks and finally arrive in Horseshoe Basin at timberline beneath Red Mountain which lies to the south southwest. Coming back down, Bald Mountain will be seen to the northeast and the mountains of the Tenmile Range to the west and northwest.

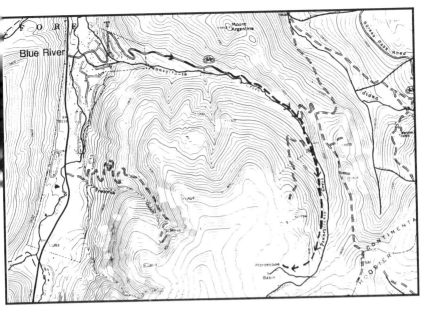

1B Peru Creek Road to Cinnamon Gulch

Tour Distance: 3.8 miles each way
Tour Time: Up in 95 minutes. Down in 66 minutes.
Starting Elevation: 10,020 feet
Highest Elevation: 10,880 feet (3316 meters)
Elevation Gain: 910 feet (includes an extra 25 feet each way)
Avalanche Danger: Moderate
Difficulty: Easiest
Steepness Index: 0.04
Trail: All the way
Relevant Maps: Montezuma 7½ minute
                       Trails Illustrated Number 104
                       Summit County Number Two
                       Arapaho National Forest (Dillon Ranger District)

Getting There: Drive on U.S. 6 either 7.7 miles east from Exit 205 of Interstate 70 or 8.5 miles south from Loveland Pass and turn south onto the road to the Keystone Ski Area. Within 50 yards make the first possible left and follow the Montezuma Road for 4.8 miles and park in the large area on the left at the trailhead. Regular cars can come this far.

The Peru Creek Road ascends gradually, surrounded by high peaks, into Horseshoe Basin. It makes a great, easy ski tour. On the way remnants of old mines dot the landscape.

Begin your tour to the northwest on the wide road. After 1.0 mile keep left at a fork and cross Peru Creek. The road then ascends more steeply for about 150 yards. This area may be icy and require special negotiation. After 0.3 miles from the creek crossing, you will pass some old mine buildings

11

and 0.4 miles later the Lenawee Trailhead is passed. Continue parallel to the power lines for another 0.4 miles and arrive at an open area with Warden Gulch and a sign on your right. Proceed east up the left fork on the main road with Cooper Mountain and then Ruby Mountain on your left and Argentine Peak ahead. After 1.7 miles from the Warden Gulch sign you will pass to the left of the power poles and arrive at a fork and a white diamond sign on a short wooden pole. To the right is Cinnamon Gulch and the ruins of the Pennsylvania Mine which you might want to explore. The left fork continues up into Horseshoe Basin. The return trip provides a gentle descent with fine vistas to the west.

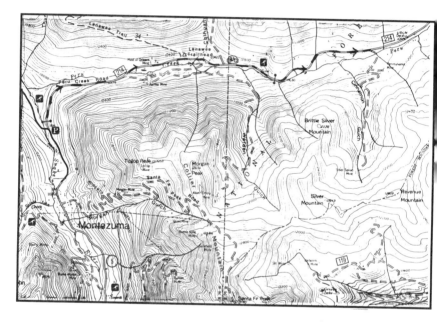

Courtesy of Trails Illustrated

2A Spruce Creek Road to Mohawk Lakes Trailhead

Tour Distance:	3.6 miles each way
Tour Time:	Up in 87 minutes. Down in 45 minutes.
Starting Elevation:	9,930 feet
Highest Elevation:	11,100 feet (3383 meters)
Elevation Gain:	1,290 feet (includes 60 extra feet each way)
Avalanche Danger:	Least
Difficulty:	More Difficult
Steepness Index:	0.07
Trail:	All the way
Relevant Maps:	Breckenridge 7½ minute
	Trails Illustrated Number 109
	Summit County Number Two
	Arapaho National Forest (Dillon Ranger District)

Getting There: From the stop light at Main Street (Colorado 9) and Ski Hill Road in Breckenridge, drive south on Colorado 9 for 2.7 miles to a road ascending to the right at a sign for "The Crown." Park here off the road. (Some vehicles can ascend the icy Spruce Creek Road for 0.8 miles before parking.)

The Spruce Creek Road is wide and for the most part gradual on its ascent to the Mohawk Lakes Trailhead. Mount Helen looms ahead of you on your ascent and Bald Mountain on the descent. There are several trails and roads off the Spruce Creek Road.

Ascend west from Colorado 9 and stay on the main road (County Road 800). Keep right at two forks within the first tenth of a mile. Then go left at a fork in 0.2 miles from Colorado 9 and take another left 0.3 miles farther as the road curves to the south. Then in rapid succession take a right, a left and a right fork before reaching the Spruce Creek Trailhead on the left side of the road after 1.3 miles from Colorado 9. Continue up the road to a fork and signs. Go left and avoid the 4-wheel drive road to Lower Crystal Lake on the right. In 0.4 miles farther, cross Crystal Creek and in 0.6 miles more reach a 4-way trail intersection. The Wheeler Trail leads to the left and right. You continue straight (southwest) and after ascending a gentle hill descend to a crossing of Spruce Creek and then climb more steeply to reach the end of the road at a small dam and a trail sign on your right. The descent provides many moderate downhill runs and opportunity to work on your technique.

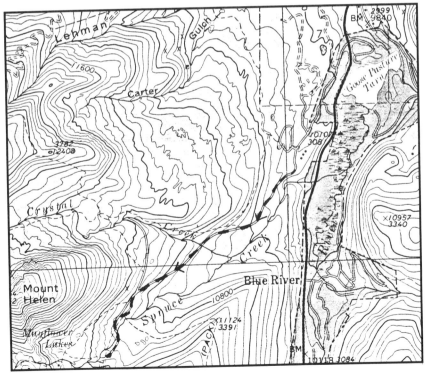

Courtesy of Trails Illustrated

13

2B Montgomery Pass

Tour Distance: 1.9 miles each way
Tour Time: Up in 76 minutes. Down in 45 minutes.
Starting Elevation: 9,990 feet
Highest Elevation: 10,990 feet (3350 meters)
Elevation Gain: 1,110 feet (includes 55 extra feet each way)
Avalanche Danger: Moderate
Difficulty: Most Difficult
Steepness Index: 0.11
Trail: All the way
Relevant Maps: Clark Peak 7½ minute
                      Trails Illustrated Number 112
                      Larimer County Number Three
                      Roosevelt National Forest

Getting There: From northwest of Fort Collins where U.S. 287 heads northwest toward Wyoming and Colorado 14 begins its long westerly ascent of lovely Poudre Canyon, drive 56.8 miles on Colorado 14 and park on the left in the Zimmerman Lake parking area. Cameron Pass is 1.5 miles farther up Colorado 14.

The higher elevations off Colorado 14 offer many scenic ski tours and make the 135 mile drive from Denver worthwhile. The tour to Montgomery Pass is one of the more difficult routes in this book. You ascend a steep, narrow road with many curves and emerge into a clearing to traverse gradual terrain to the pass.

This tour begins across the road from the parking area past a tree with a blue diamond marker. Enter the trees to the north northwest and ascend steeply as the narrow trail curves back to the left. Be prepared for a lot of herring bone or side-stepping maneuvers. After 1.5 miles from the trailhead you will reach a small clearing. Some tracks will be leading steeply upward to your left (southwest). Avoid that route and continue west on a trail into the trees. Soon a blue diamond tree marker will confirm your choice. After a short descent to cross a drainage you will rise to a large treeless area and then head southwest toward the pass. This area is often quite windy. A prominent wooden sign marks Montgomery Pass. The view of North Park to the southwest is impressive as are the many snowcapped peaks in every direction. The return to Colorado 14 is rapid and requires lots of control and discretion.

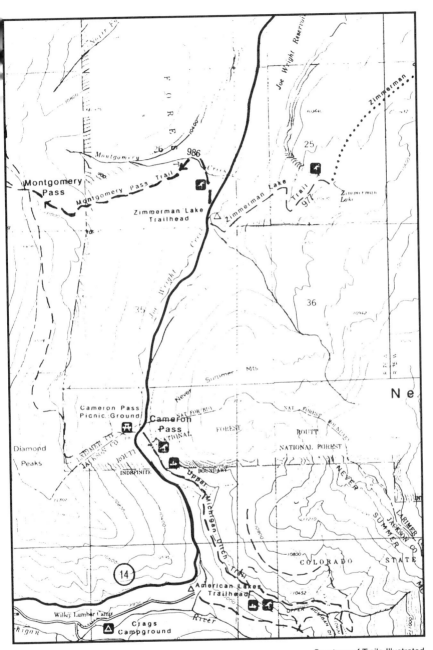

Courtesy of Trails Illustrated

3A Shrine Pass to Redcliff

Tour Distance:	10.4 miles (total one way)
Tour Time:	Trailhead (near Vail Pass) to Shrine Pass in 49 minutes. Shrine Pass to Redcliff in 107 minutes. (Total 156 minutes)
Starting Elevation:	10,600 feet
Highest Elevation:	11,165 feet (3403 meters)
Elevation Gain:	730 feet (includes an extra 165 feet)
Avalanche Danger:	Moderate
Difficulty:	More Difficult
Steepness Index:	0.05
Trail:	All the way
Relevant Maps:	Vail Pass 7½ minute
	Red Cliff 7½ minute
	Trails Illustrated Number 108
	Trails Illustrated Cross-Country Skier's Map Number 403
	Summit County Number Two
	Eagle County Number Four
	Arapaho National Forest
	White River National Forest

Getting There: Drive two cars to Redcliff off U.S. 24 as follows: From Exit 171 of Interstate 70 west of Vail, drive south on U.S. 24 through Minturn for a total of 10.5 miles to a road leading to Redcliff on the left just before you reach a large bridge. Descend for 0.6 miles on this good road into Redcliff and then turn left onto the Shrine Pass Road and continue east for 1.1 miles to the end of the ploughed road and a parking area on your right at a water tank. Leave one car here and retrace your route to Interstate 70. Follow I-70 east through Vail and just east of Vail Pass, exit to the right and reach the Shrine Pass Road and an extensive parking area just off I-70 to the west. The Shrine Pass Road begins about 200 yards west of I-70 on the north edge of the access road. The distance from Redcliff to the Shrine Pass exit and parking area is 30 miles via Interstate 70.

The Shrine Pass Road is perhaps the best ski tour in Colorado. The usual tactic is to have a car at each end of the route and to ski from east to west. This way is mostly downhill and affords views of Mount of the Holy Cross. Try this trek on a weekday if you want to avoid the crowds of skiers and snowmobilers.

Begin south southwest from the national forest sign and after a few switchbacks continue northwest up the road. You will reach the high point with some rocky outcroppings on your right in 1.7 miles and Shrine Pass, which is somewhat lower, at a White River National Forest sign in another half mile. The Shrine Mountain Inn can be seen in the woods south of the pass. You will then gradually descend southwest through mostly open valley. Avoid the occasional side roads and continue on the road bed along Turkey Creek. In the middle third of the tour there is some avalanche terrain above to your right. About four miles below the pass there are two abandoned cabins on your left. This area is ideal for a lunch break. The descent soon becomes a bit steeper before levelling out for the final stretch to your car at the water tank parking area. The Reno Cafe in Redcliff is a popular watering hole for nordic skiers after this tour.

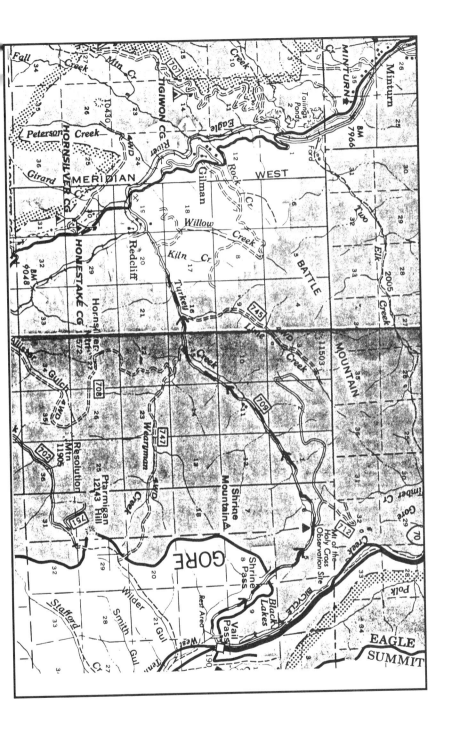

3B Rabbit Ears Peak

Tour Distance:	3.4 miles each way
Tour Time:	Up in 100 minutes. Down in 68 minutes.
Starting Elevation:	9,425 feet (East Rabbit Ears Pass).
Highest Elevation:	10,550 feet (3216 meters)
Elevation Gain:	1,305 feet (includes 90 feet extra each way)
Avalanche Danger:	Significant
Difficulty:	Most Difficult
Steepness Index:	0.07
Trail:	All the way
Relevant Maps:	Rabbit Ears Pass 7½ minute
	Trails Illustrated Number 118
	Grand County Number One
	Jackson County Number Three
	Routt National Forest

Getting There: Drive to East Rabbit Ears Pass on U.S. 40 and park on the north side of the road near the pass sign. This point is 3.2 miles northwest of the intersection of Colorado 14 with U.S. 40 or 21.5 miles southeast of the intersection of Third Street with U.S. 40 (Lincoln Avenue) in Steamboat Springs.

Here is a tour which is shared with snowmobilers. However, you pass through several open meadows with plenty of room for everyone. The peak can be seen throughout most of the tour and when you leave the road, you can follow tracks up to the final road which approaches the summit from the left (west). You finish at the foot of rocky Rabbit Ears Peak and the views are fantastic. There are no trail markers en route.

Start your tour from the left of the East Rabbit Ears Pass sign annd gradually ascend northwest through a large open meadow. In a half mile reach a road which enters the trees. Follow this bumpy road another 0.8 miles to a four-way intersection at a stone marker for the old Rabbit Ears Pass. Continue straight (north) on the road. After a half mile from the large rock marker you enter another large open meadow with a single burnt tree trunk at its upper north-west area. Keep to the right of this trunk and either continue north through some trees or pass around to your right (northeast) to gain an even larger open bowl with Rabbit Ears Peak to the north northeast. Ascend the bowl northwest and then curve to the north. Head for a clearing in the trees above the bowl and to the left of Rabbit Ears Peak. Ascend steeply to this point and then follow the road in a counterclockwise direction to the foot of the summit rocks. The last mile of this ascent is the most steep. Forget about going to the very top of the two summit blocks. They would require difficult rock scrambling with hiking boots. Admire the great views before your extensive downhill glide retracing your route back to the trailhead.

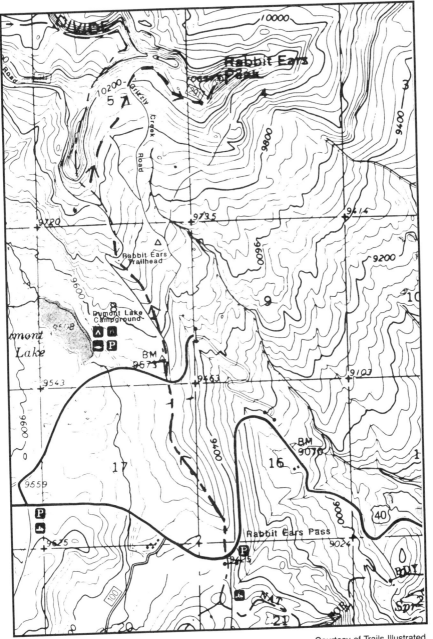

Courtesy of Trails Illustrated

4A Crooked Creek Road to Crystal Creek

Tour Distance: 5.5 miles each way
Tour Time: Up in 120 minutes. Down in 94 minutes.
Starting Elevation: 8,780 feet
Highest Elevation: 9,270 feet (2859 meters)
Elevation Gain: 640 feet (includes 75 feet extra each way)
Avalanche Danger: Least
Difficulty: More Difficult
Steepness Index: 0.02
Trail: All the way
Relevant Maps: Fraser 7½ minute
                      Bottle Pass 7½ minute
                      Trails Illustrated Number 103
                      Grand County Number Four
                      Arapaho National Forest

Getting There: From the stop light in Fraser, drive north on U.S. 40 for 0.9 miles. Turn left and cross the railroad tracks. After 0.2 miles from U.S. 40, take a left fork and follow the Crooked Creek Road for 3.0 miles to the end of county maintenance and park on the right just before a cattle guard. En route to this point stay on the main route and avoid connecting secondary roads.

The Crooked Creek Road, also called the Church Park Road, northwest of Fraser, provides a long, level ski tour up a beautiful valley in the Arapaho National Forest. Some snowmobiles may be encountereed, especially on weekend days.

Begin on the road to the southwest from your parking area. The first part of the tour meanders without much change in elevation. Avoid side trails and stay on the wide, main road. After 2.6 miles you will reach a fork at a bend in the road. You continue to the right as the left fork ascends along Tipperary Creek and provides a more demanding ski tour. After 2.2 more miles, a large clearing and overlook is reached. The gentle slopes to your left are off the road and can be used for downhill runs. To the north Rocky Point and Sheep Mountain can be seen. Continue west on the road for 0.7 more miles to a smaller clearing where Crystal Creek passes under the road. This is the destination of your tour. (The road continues 2.9 miles into Church Park and beyond.) The return trip involves several gentle downhill runs.

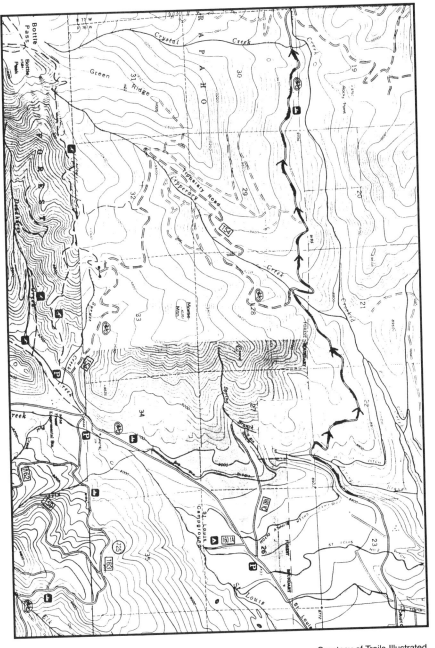

Courtesy of Trails Illustrated

21

4B Boreas Pass from Breckenridge

Tour Distance:	6.6 miles each way
Tour Time:	Up in 150 minutes. Down in 114 minutes.
Starting Elevation:	10,350 feet
Highest Elevation:	11,481 feet (3499 meters)
Elevation Gain:	1,143 feet (includes an extra 6 feet each way)
Avalanche Danger:	Moderate
Difficulty:	More Difficult
Steepness Index:	0.03
Trail:	All the way
Relevant Maps:	Breckenridge 7½ minute
	Boreas Pass 7½ minute
	Trails Illustrated Number 109
	Trails Illustrated Cross-Country Skier's Map Number 401
	Summit County Number Two
	Arapaho National Forest (Dillon Ranger District)

Getting There: From the stop light in Breckenridge at Ski Hill Road and Lincoln Avenue, drive south on Colorado 9 for 0.6 miles and turn left onto the Boreas Pass Road. Stay on the main road which is Summit County Road Number 10 for 3.75 more miles to the end of the plowed road and park. En route to this point avoid various minor side roads and keep left, right and right at the three major forks.

High mountain passes make great ski tour destinations. They often have old roads over them, are near timberline, and afford great vistas. Boreas Pass is named after the God of the North Wind. The Denver, South Park and Pacific Narrow Gauge Railroad connected Como with Breckenridge by way of Boreas Pass. The track was completed in 1884 and the line operated until 1937. A town called Boreas was located at the pass and provided lodging and services for railroad workers and travelers.

From the parking area, ski up the road and pass a metal gate in about 100 yards. Continue up the shelf road which generally continues southeast along the western flank of Bald Mountain. An old water tower, Bakers Tank, is passed on the left in 60 minutes from the trailhead. Continue southeast up the road and eventually bypass a side road on the right to Indiana and Pennsylvania Creeks. The pass is reached in 90 minutes from Bakers Tank. Some abandoned buildings lie on the left (east) side of the pass. This is your destination. (The road continues southeast for 11 more miles to Como and U.S. 285 beyond.)

On your continuous, gradual descent, the peaks of the Tenmile Range are impressive to the northwest.

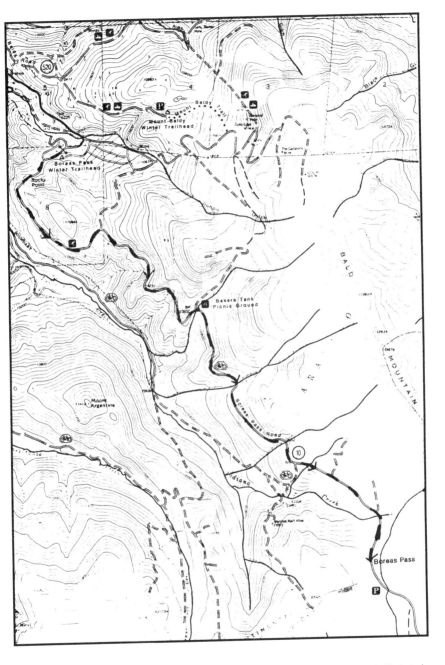

Courtesy of Trails Illustrated

5A Peaks Trail: Breckenridge to Frisco

Tour Distance: 8.5 miles one way
Tour Time: Down in 177 minutes
Starting Elevation: 10,030 feet
Highest Elevation: 10,240 feet (3121 meters)
Elevation Gain: 765 feet (includes 555 extra feet)
Avalanche Danger: Moderate
Difficulty: Most Difficult
Steepness Index: 0.02
Trail: All the way
Relevant Maps: Breckenridge 7½ minute
                      Frisco 7½ minute
                      Trails Illustrated Cross-Country Skier's Map Number 401
                      Trails Illustrated Numbers 108 and 109
                      Summit County Number Two
                      Arapaho National Forest—Dillon Ranger District

Getting There: This tour requires two cars: one at each end of this route. Drive one car south from Main Street in Frisco on Colorado 9 for 0.5 miles and turn right. (A maintenance facility will be on your left after your turn). Take an immediate right fork and after 0.1 mile more keep right again and drive another tenth of a mile and park at a road barrier and a Miners Creek Trail sign. Drive the second car further south on Colorado 9 to Ski Hill Road and a traffic light in Breckenridge. Turn right on Ski Hill Road and follow it a total of 2.3 miles and park in a designated area on the left just past a Peaks Trail sign at the trailhead. En route to this point on Ski Hill Road pass the Nordic Center on the right and take a right fork at 0.7 miles from Colorado 9 and drive past the Peak 8 parking areas and curve up the hill before decending to the trailhead. Regular cars can reach both the Frisco and the Breckenridge Trailheads.

This is one of those Colorado ski tours which you will hear about a great deal and sooner or later you will probably want to try. The tour covers lots of beautiful terrain but offers difficulties with good length, lots of ups and downs and some narrow and curving downhill sections, especially in the second half of the tour If you want to try it with only one car, drive to the Breckenridge trailhead and then use the free ski shuttle from Frisco back to the Peak 8 parking area and walk the final 1.3 miles back to your car. (Shuttle information is widely available in Frisco and Breckenridge.) The tour leads mostly through the trees, crosses several creeks and offers occasional views of the Tenmile Range on the left and of Grays Peak, Torreys Peak, Bald Mountain and Mount Argentine on the right. The descent from the Breckenridge Trailhead to the Frisco Trailhead is 1,740 feet.

Begin skiing west northwest into the trees from the Breckenridge trailhead. In 0.9 miles you will reach a 4 way intersection at Cucumber Creek. Continue straight (north) and follow the blue diamond trail markers on the trees. In the next two and a half miles you will cross South, Middle and North Barton Creeks as the trail rises and falls. After a quarter mile past North Barton Creek you will reach a clearing which slopes downward to the east. This is a scenic halfway point for a lunch break. Resume northward for another 1.1 miles to a four way intersection at several trail signs. The Miners Creek Trail and the Colorado Trail lead to the left. You continue straight toward

Rainbow Lake and in 0.7 miles pass the Gold Hill Trail on the right. It is 2.1 more miles of creek crossings and steep downhill sections until you reach the plowed Miners Creek Road near Rainbow Lake. Follow the road down to the right (north northwest) and in 0.4 miles stay on the main road as it turns sharply and descends to the left. You quickly reach a T and go left. (This is the summer bike path.) In a few hundred yards you reach a five way intersection. Take the second right road down to your vehicle at the Frisco trailhead.

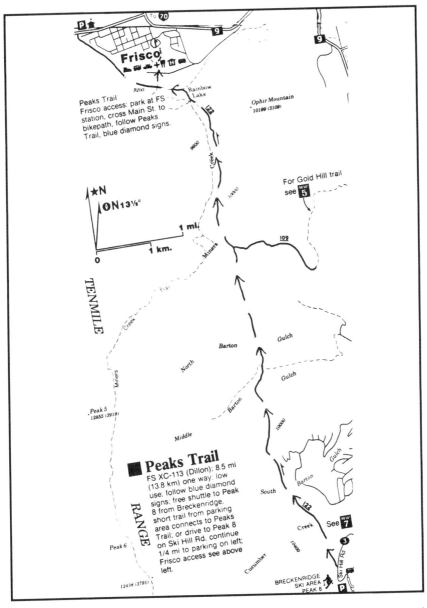

Courtesy of Trails Illustrated

5B   North Rock Creek

Tour Distance:	3.6 miles each way
Tour Time:	Up in 67 minutes. Back in 67 minutes
Starting Elevation:	8,875
Highest Elevation:	9,590 feet (2923 meters)
Elevation Gain:	915 feet
Avalanche Danger:	Least
Difficulty:	Easiest
Steepness Index:	0.05
Trail:	All the way
Relevant Maps:	Willow Lakes 7½ minute
	Trails Illustrated Number 108
	Summit County Numbers One and Two
	Arapaho National Forest

Getting There: From exit 205 from Interstate 70, drive north on Colorado 9 for 7.7 miles and turn left onto the Rock Creek Road. (This turnoff is almost opposite the Blue River Campground.) Drive up the Rock Creek Road for 1.4 miles and park in the designated area on your left. This area lies 100 yards past a fork sign which indicates that Rock Creek is to the left and just past the entrance to Pebble Creek Ranch on the other side of the road. Some cars may have difficulty ascending the Rock Creek Road. If so, park in the open area just off Colorado 9 and hike or ski up the road to the parking area.

This ski tour up North Rock Creek is in a less known and used area. The grade is gentle up to an abandoned cabin to the east of Keller Mountain in the Eagles Nest Wilderness.

Start from the parking area to the east southeast and descend to the Rock Creek Road. Turn right and ski parallel to North Rock Creek which will always be on your left. In a half mile keep right and on the road as it meanders to the southwest. In 1.4 miles farther you will reach the Rock Creek Trailhead sign. Take the left fork and ascend onto the Rock Creek Trail and past a trail register on your left. Very quickly you will then pass a wilderness sign and a metal road barrier. Within a half mile from this barrier, you will cross Gore Range Trail. Continue southwest on the Rock Creek Trail and in a quarter mile after the Gore Range Trail intersection, pass a sign on your left for the Alfred M. Bailey Bird Nesting Area. In 0.3 more miles arrive at a fork and descend left into a large open area with an abandoned stone cabin at its far end. This cabin is the terminus for this ski tour. If you want a longer outing, go right at the last fork and ascend more steeply for another 1.3 miles to reach some remnants of the former Boss Mine. Retrace your ascent route for the glide back to your vehicle.

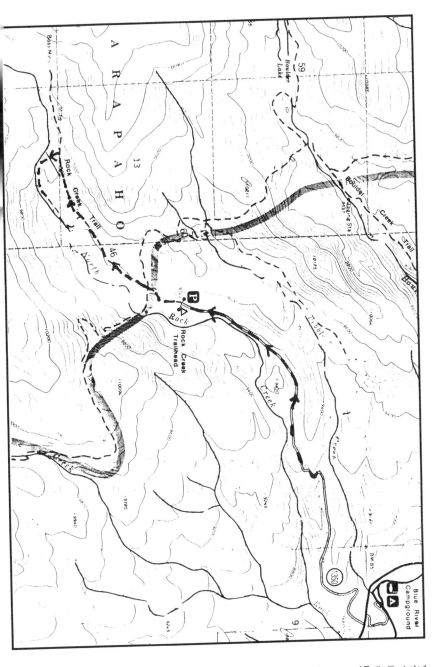

6A Fourth of July Road To Buckingham Campground

Tour Distance:	4.9 miles each way
Tour Time:	Up in 130 minutes. Down in 100 minutes
Starting Elevation:	8,820
Highest Elevation:	10,170 feet (3100 meters)
Elevation Gain:	1,426 feet (includes 38 feet extra each way)
Avalanche Danger:	Least
Difficulty:	More difficult (due to length)
Steepness Index:	0.05
Trail:	All the way
Relevant Maps:	Nederland 7½ minute
	East Portal 7½ minute
	Trails Illustrated Number 102
	Boulder County
	Roosevelt National Forest

Getting There: Drive on Colorado 119 about 20 miles west of Boulder to the town of Nederland. From the intersection with Colorado 72 in Nederland, drive south on Colorado 119 for 0.6 miles and turn right onto Boulder County Road 130. On this road keep right at mile 1.4 and again at mile 2.5. Drive through the town of Eldora on the main road and park at mile 4.0 on the western edge of town where road maintenance ends. Be sure to park off the road and not to block other vehicles.

This ski tour takes you into the beautiful Indian Peaks area. You will ski on a wide, gradually ascending road which ends at the Buckingham Campground and the trailhead to Arapaho Pass and Diamond Lake. The road can be icy in the first half mile and is frequently windswept. The best time period for this tour is from mid January through February.

Start skiing up the Fourth of July Road to the west northwest. After 0.8 miles, reach a fork and signs. Go right and generally ascend to the northwest along the north fork of Middle Boulder Creek. In 2.5 miles from the fork keep left on the main road and pass a single cabin on your left. You traverse several clearings and, near the end, pass several cabins before reaching your destination, the Buckingham Campground and a road barrier near trail signs. South Arapaho Peak lies up ahead to the northwest. Your lengthy but gentle descent should take around two-thirds of the time required to ascend.

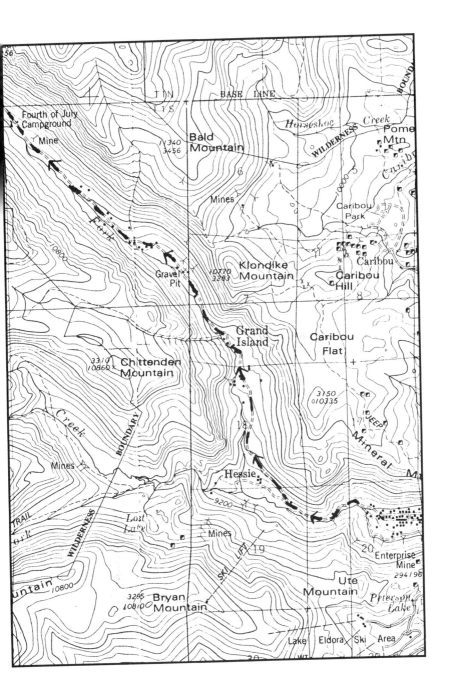

6B Lily Lake (Lake County)

Tour Distance:	3.1 miles each way
Tour Time:	Up in 75 minutes. Down in 50 minutes
Starting Elevation:	10,137
Highest Elevation:	10,589 feet (3090 meters)
Elevation Gain:	552 feet (includes an extra 50 feet each way)
Avalanche Danger:	Least
Difficulty:	More difficult
Steepness Index:	0.03
Trail:	All the way
Relevant Maps:	Leadville North 7½ minute
	Trails Illustrated Number 109
	Lake County
	San Isabel National Forest

Getting There: From the intersection of Colorado 91 and U.S. 24 north of Leadville, drive northwest on U.S. 24 for 7.1 miles, turn left and park within 100 yards near a trail sign on the right side of the road.

Lily Lake, northwest of Leadville, makes a fine destination for a ski tour. The terrain gradually rises, the trail is wide and the scenery beautiful with Homestake Peak and the Continental Divide looming above to the northwest. There is a loop trail which provides a return route from the south side of Lily Lake but this alternate trail will not be described here.

Begin on the road from your parking area and proceed west southwest. The initial parts of this road may be icy. The road winds up past some homes into the trees and in one mile brings you to a fork in the road. Go left and avoid the sign to the Lily Lake Loop which directs you to the right. In 0.3 miles from the fork, pass a Colorado Trail sign and continue west northwest past some old, wooden buildings on the right. In 0.6 miles, after the Colorado Trail sign, continue straight at a 4-way intersection at a trail sign. The trail becomes a bit steeper from here to the lake and in about one more mile from the 4-way intersection you will reach another fork. The right fork is part of the 10th Mountain Trail. You go left and within one hundred yards reach tranquil, frozen Lily Lake on your left, cradled in a ring of trees. Enjoy the gentle downhill slopes as you return by way of your ascent route.

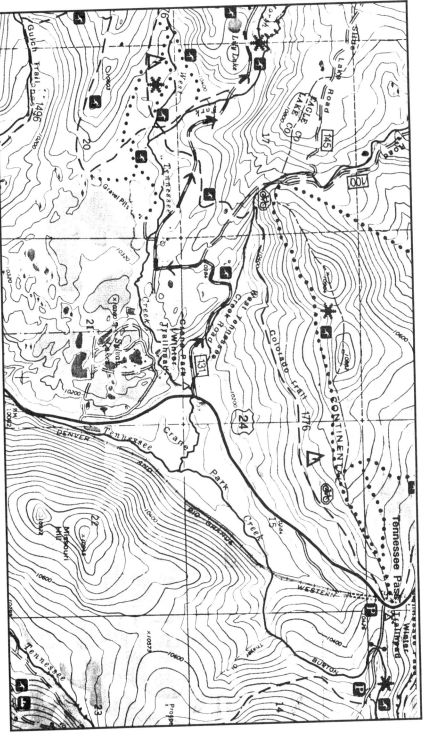

31

7A. Urad Lake

Tour Distance:	3.1 miles each way
Tour Time:	Up in 88 minutes. Down in 57 minutes
Starting Elevation:	9,950 feet
Highest Elevation:	10,740 feet (3274 meters)
Elevation Gain:	940 feet (includes an extra 75 feet each way)
Avalanche Danger:	Moderate
Difficulty:	More difficult
Steepness Index:	0.06
Trail:	All the way
Relevant Maps:	Berthoud Pass 7½ minute
	Grays Peak 7½ minute
	Trails Illustrated Numbers 103 and 104
	Clear Creek County
	Arapaho National Forest

Getting There: From Interstate 70, take exit 232 onto U.S. 40, pass through the town of Empire and drive a total of 9.3 miles. Then take a left turn onto the access road to the Henderson Mine. Turn left again in 0.1 mile from U.S. 40, and in 0.4 miles farther turn left onto the road to the Urad Reclamation Area. Follow this road for 0.25 miles until the ploughed area ends and park at a fork with a metal barrier on the left.

The ski tour to Urad Lake is not widely known. It involves a gradual ascent with a few steeper parts up an old mining road to Urad Lake. The valley is ringed with beautiful snowcapped peaks and the ski traffic in the valley should be sparse. This area catches a great deal of wind and sometimes parts of the road will have little snow cover.

Begin south from the parking area by passing over the bank of ploughed snow onto an ascending area. After touring up the valley for 1.3 miles, take a left fork. In 0.3 more miles take a right fork and in 0.3 more miles take a left fork. Always avoid going through or around any closed metal gates. A tour of 0.3 more miles brings you through an open gate at a Urad Lake sign. Follow the road then as it ascends more steeply to the right. After reaching the top of the bank pass down slightly through an open valley. In 0.8 miles more, take a right fork at a wooden sign and ascend southwest into the trees. A tenth of a mile later take a left fork and ascend a shelf road which reaches an overlook of Urad Lake at a sign. The lake will lie below to the west and the impressive, rocky summit of Red Mountain can be seen to the north northeast. As you retrace your ascent route and glide back to your car, Colorado Mines Peak, with buildings on its summit, will be visible to the northeast.

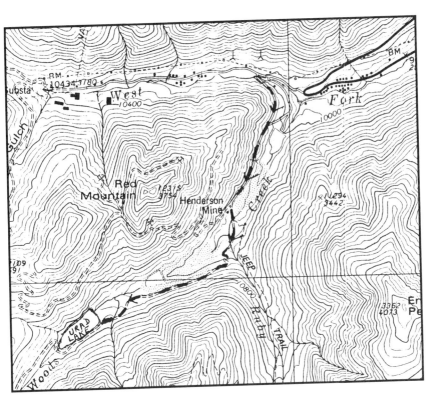

7B. Brainard Lake Loop (CMC South and Waldrop Ski Trails)

Tour Distance: 7.0 miles (total loop)
Tour Time: Out in 89 minutes. Back in 76 minutes. (loop)
Starting Elevation: 10,080 feet
Highest Elevation: 10,475 feet (3193 meters)
Elevation Gain: 10,475 feet (includes 102 extra feet on the CMC South Trail and 265 extra feet on the Waldrop Trail)
Avalanche Danger: Least
Difficulty: More Difficult
Steepness Index: 0.04
Trail: All the way
Relevant Maps: Ward 7½ minute
Trails Illustrated Number 102
Trails Illustrated Cross-Country Skier's Map Number 402
Boulder County
Roosevelt National Forest

Getting There: From its intersectioon with Colorado 119 at the eastern edge of Nederland, drive north 12.1 miles on Colorado 72 and turn left onto the Brainard Lake Road. Follow this excellent road for 2.6 miles and park near the road barrier. This is the Red Rock Trailhead.

The Red Rock Trailhead, west of Ward, offers a large selection of ski touring trails into the eastern slopes of the Indian Peaks. Due to heavy winds occasional bare areas may be encountered. This loop trail forbids dogs and snowmobiles and can be skied in either direction. The easier leg is the CMC South Ski Trail which is reached by way of the Left Hand Reservoir Road. This trail proceeds west following blue diamond markers on the trees. At the southwestern end of Brainard Lake you will briefly join the road encircling the lake and then ascend toward the Mitchell Lake Trailhead. Before that trailhead is reached, the Waldrop Ski Trail leads off to the right and returns east through some steeper areas to the trailhead. An alternative, easier return from Brainard Lake is via the road back to the barrier at the Red Rock Trailhead.

Start your tour by going south on the Left Hand Reservoir Road which is 100 yards east of the barrier on the Brainard Lake Road. Ski past another barrier on this road and ascend a quarter of a mile to a fork and a sign. Take the right fork into the trees. This is the CMC South Ski Trail. Within 100 yards take a left fork and continue west following the blue diamond markers. After 3.25 miles you will reach a fork and some signs. The Little Raven Trail goes left but you descend to the right and reach the road around Brainard Lake. Continue northwest past the Niwot Mountain Picnic Ground and in 200 yards farther ascend to the left at a fork. In 200 more yards keep right (north) at another fork and continue toward the Mitchell Lake Trailhead. Pass a sign on the right for the Waldrop Trail and the CMC Cabin and continue on the road another 100 yards to a second Waldrop Trail sign on the right. This is the far point of the tour. Follow this trail, which is also the South St. Vrain Ski Trail, to the east northeast through an open wind-blown area to a fork at the high point of this loop. Descend via the left fork through the trees and after a quarter mile take another left fork. Another quarter mile brings you to a fork and a sign. The left fork continues as the South St. Vrain Trail. You go right on the Waldrop Trail, cross South St. Vrain Creek and avoid a right fork to the Brainard Lake Road at the top of a clearing. Continue east as the trail rises and falls. Keep left at two consecutive forks and finally reach the Brainard Lake Road about 300 yards west of the road barrier and the trailhead.

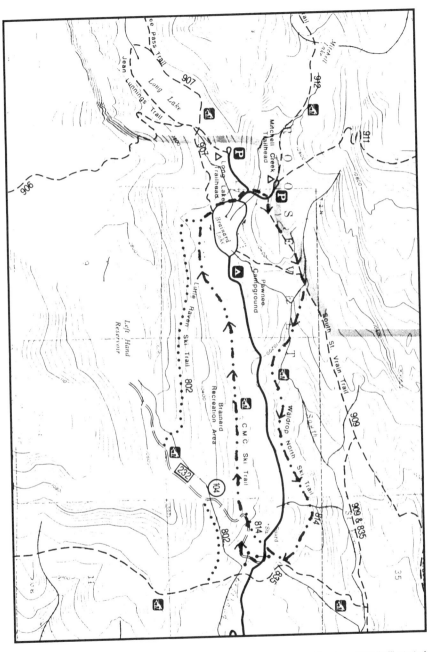

Courtesy of Trails Illustrated

35

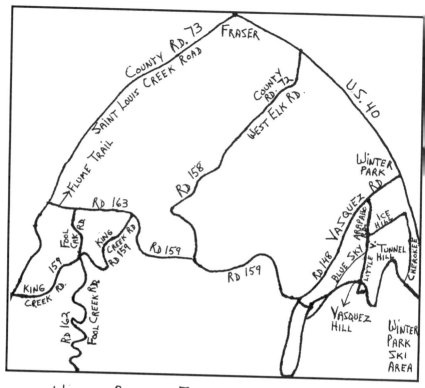

WINTER PARK — FRASER NORDIC TRAILS

8A Little Vasquez – Cherokee Trail Loop

Tour Distance: 4.5 miles (total loop)
Tour Time: Up in 70 minutes. Down in 30 minutes.
Starting Elevation: 8,970 feet
Highest Elevation: 9,600 feet (2926 meters)
Elevation Gain: 725 feet (includes 95 extra feet)
Avalanche Danger: Moderate
Difficulty: More Difficult
Steepness Index: 0.03
Trail: All the way
Relevant Maps: Fraser 7½ minute
             Grand County Number Four
             Arapaho National Forest
             Trails Illustrated Number 103

Getting There: Drive on U.S. 40 to the Vasquez Road in Winter Park. This turnoff is 13.4 miles north of Berthoud Pass. Follow the Vasquez Road west over the railroad tracks for 0.4 miles from U.S. 40 and turn left on Arapaho Road. Stay on Arapaho Road for 0.4 miles until it ends just past a four-way intersection at the Little Vasquez Trail sign. Park in the area designated by the signs.

Here is a tour in the wonderful network of free trails south and west of Winter Park. You will cross many intersections and therefore have many other trails to explore either on this or subsequent tours. One steep downhill run, a sometimes steep ascent through the trees, a wide mountain road and great views are all found in this loop.

Start skiing south southeast on the Little Vasquez Trail and avoid two side roads on your left near the trailhead. After 1000 feet take a sharp left fork leading north northeast. This is the Ice Hill Trail. Take two consecutive right forks and after 0.8 miles on the Ice Hill Trail reach a steep, straight downhill run. Descend this according to your ability. Continue east and keep right at two forks before reaching a T and the Tracks Trail at a sign. (The railroad tracks lie nearby to the east.)

Go right (south southeast) for 0.2 miles and take a right (south) fork up the Cherokee Trail. Ascend somewhat steeply for 1.2 miles to a T at a level road. Take the right fork and ascend west northwest on the main road and in 0.7 miles reach the high point of the Tunnel Hill Trail and this tour. There are many good vistas of the Winter Park downhill ski slopes and the Fraser Valley. Continue the loop by descending 0.3 miles to a fork. Go down the right fork and keep left within 200 yards as a side trail descends to the right. In another 200 yards you will arrive at a four-way intersection. Turn right (north) and enjoy the glide back to the trailhead on the Little Vasquez Trail as you pass under a large water pipe and past two utility buildings. Stay on the main trail all the way.

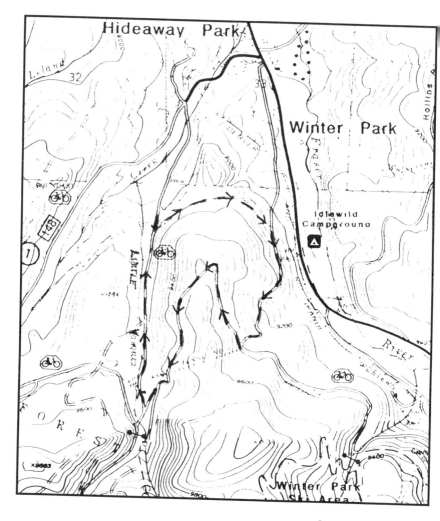

8B West Rabbit Ears Pass – North Loop

Tour Distance: 3.5 miles (total loop)
Tour Time: Up in 70 minutes. Down in 20 minutes. (loop)
Starting Elevation: 9,320 feet
Highest Elevation: 9,618 feet (2932 meters)
Elevation Gain: 418 feet (includes an extra 120 feet)
Avalanche Danger: Least
Difficulty: Easiest
Steepness Index: 0.05
Trail: All the way
Relevant Maps: Walton Peak 7½ minute
                     Mount Werner 7½ minute
                     Trails Illustrated Number 118
                     Routt County Number Four
                     Routt National Forest

38

Getting There: Drive to West Rabbit Ears Pass on U.S. 40 and park in the designated area on the north side of the highway. This is 10.8 miles northwest of the intersection of Colorado 14 with U.S. 40 or 13.9 miles southeast of 3rd Street and U.S. 40 (Lincoln Avenue) in Steamboat Springs.

The area between East and West Rabbit Ears Passes is full of wonderful tours for all levels of skiers. This winter playground has many signs and is covered with large open meadows for free skiing. There is much snowmobile traffic in the area.

Start this tour to the north from the parking area past two trail signs. Within 100 yards take the right fork and descend. After another 300 yards, keep right at another fork and continue down to a low point at a fork and trail symbol. To your left is a vast rising meadow. Go right (east northeast) and follow the blue diamond markers parallel to U.S. 40 which lies on your right. After 0.6 miles from the last fork reach a trail sign and another fork. To the right is the Walton Creek Overlook Trail. You take the left fork and ascend northwest through an open meadow. Keep in the drainage and rise to a high flat area with great views in all directions except to the northeast. Mount Werner lies to the north, Hahns Peak to the northwest and Walton Peak to the southeast. Take in the scenic beauty and some refreshment before your rapid return. Avoid the trail descending southwest and descend by trail to the south and then curve southeast for 0.7 miles from the high point back to a fork you encountered early in the tour. Go right and gradually ascend southeast and then curve to the right back to the trailhead. If you want more ski touring, there are many other choices in the area including a northwest loop between the trailhead and the high point described above.

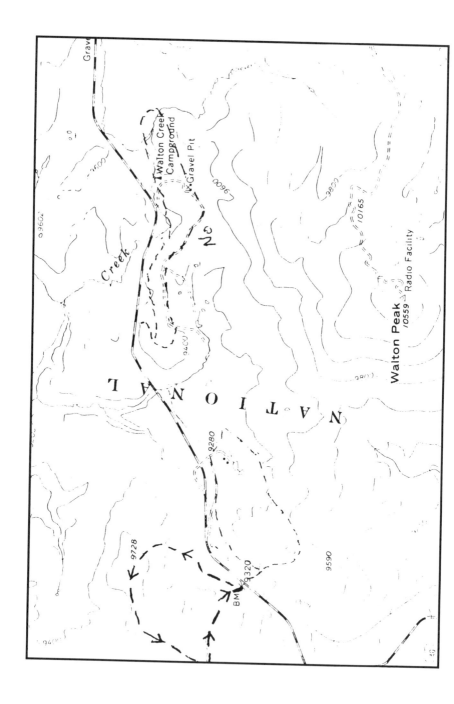

Walton Peak

10559 ▷ Radio Facility

Walton Creek
Campground

Gravel Pit

Creek

N A T I O N A L

9280

9728

BM 9320

9590

9600

7960

9400

9A Leavenworth Gulch to Waldorf

Tour Distance:	6.2 miles each way
Tour Time:	Up in 178 minutes. Down in 94 minutes
Starting Elevation:	9,560 feet
Highest Elevation:	11,594 feet (3534 meters)
Elevation Gain:	2,034 feet
Avalanche Danger:	Moderate
Difficulty:	More difficult
Steepness Index:	0.06
Trail:	All the way
Relevant Maps:	Georgetown 7½ minute
	Grays Peak 7½ minute
	Trails Illustrated Number 104
	Clear Creek County
	Arapaho National Forest

Getting There: From the middle of Georgetown (just off Interstate 70), drive south from the unmarked intersection with four stop signs adjacent to a small park and the John Tomay Memorial Library. Follow this road (which leads to Guanella Pass, Grant and U.S. 285) for 2.8 miles from the intersection in Georgetown to a bend in the road and an unpaved road (marked with a sign, Road 248), going off to the right. Park here at a large flat area off the main road.

The road up Leavenworth Gulch can be reached in about one hour from Denver. The initial segment is steep but the main shelf road provides a gentle ascent into a beautiful basin surrounded by high peaks. This tour will be strenuous due to its length.

Begin south from the parking area up the side road which has several switch-backs. Take two right forks before taking a sharp left fork and heading southwest in about 1.1 miles from the trailhead. Follow the road which runs parallel to Leavenworth Creek which will always be on your left. En route to the abandoned Waldorf Mine keep right at two more forks and never lose any elevation. Roads continue from Waldorf left to Argentine Pass and right to Mount McClellan and Ganley Mountain. Enjoy the gradual descent from the Waldorf Mine until the steeper final part of the tour. Georgetown has several fine eating places to warm you up after this good workout.

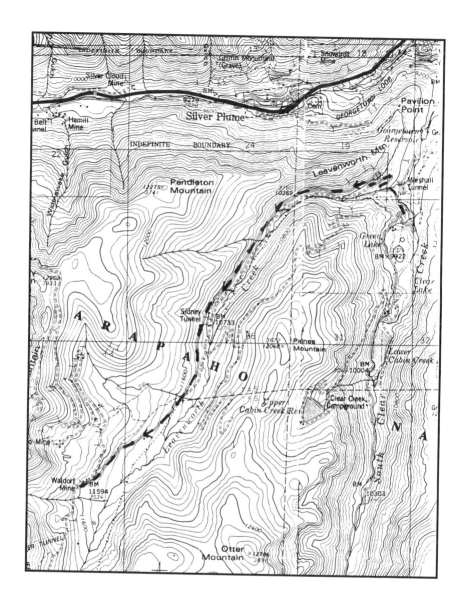

9B Saints John

Tour Distance:	1.6 miles each way
Tour Time:	Up in 34 minutes. Down in 22 minutes.
Starting Elevation:	10,300 feet
Highest Elevation:	10,760 feet (3280 meters)
Elevation Gain:	480 feet (includes an extra 10 feet each way)
Avalanche Danger:	Least
Difficulty:	More Difficult
Steepness Index:	0.06
Trail:	All the way

Relevant Maps: Montezuma 7½ minute
                      Keystone 7½ minute
                      Trails Illustrated Number 104
                      Trails Illustrated Cross-Country Skier's Map Number 401
                      Summit County Number Two
                      Arapaho National Forest (Dillon Ranger District)

Getting There: From Exit 205 from Interstate 70 at Silverthorne, drive east on U.S. 6 for 7.7 miles and turn right onto the road into the Keystone Ski Area. (This turnoff is 13.5 miles from Interstate 70 via Loveland Pass.) Within 150 feet make the first possible left turn onto the Montezuma Road and follow it for 5.7 miles into the town of Montezuma and park on the right off County Road 275 which is the road to Saints John.

Saints John was named in 1867 by some resident Freemasons after Saint John, the Baptist and Saint John, the Evangelist. These two are patron saints of freemasonry. The Saints John Mine lies above the town to the southeast and can be reached by a road leading south from town. Remnants of old mines abound in this area. During winter weekends, simple food and lodging are available at The Saints in the town of Saints John (Phone: 303-468-5378).

Start your ski tour by descending slightly and crossing a creek and then ascending south southwest. Keep right and on the main road after 0.2 miles. Soon the road will switchback twice before entering the valley and crossing Saints John Creek just prior to entry into the town. (For a longer tour you may continue southwest along Saints John Creek and then curve to the southeast for another 1.8 miles from Saints John to reach the ruins of the Wild Irishman Mine around timberline, on Glacier Mountain.) On your return which will go quickly, the two large mountains to the north northeast are Torreys and Grays Peaks.

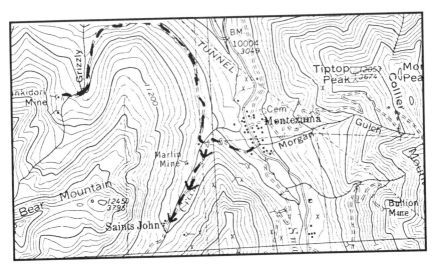

43

10A Romley

Tour Distance:	3.2 miles each way
Tour Time:	Up in 80 minutes. Down in 45 minutes.
Starting Elevation:	9,976 feet
Highest Elevation:	10,563 feet (3220 meters)
Elevation Gain:	587 feet
Avalanche Danger:	Least
Difficulty:	Easiest
Steepness Index:	0.03
Trail:	All the way (Chaffee Road 295)
Relevant Maps:	Saint Elmo 7½ minute
	Trails Illustrated Number 130
	Chaffee County Number Two
	San Isabel National Forest

Getting There: From the stop light on Main Street in Buena Vista, drive south on U.S. 24 for 2.5 miles to the intersection with U.S. 285. Continue south on U.S. 285 for 5.7 miles (past Nathrop) and turn right (west) on Chaffee 162. Stay on Chaffee 162 for 15.8 miles to a fork. The right fork continues 0.3 miles to Saint Elmo and the left fork is Chaffee 295 to Hancock. This is your trailhead. Park either 0.1 mile back or 0.1 mile farther on the right side of Chaffee 162 as it leads into Saint Elmo.

This tour, which passes above the former town site of Romley, uses the train bed to Hancock. There are ruins of old mines on the way and beautiful views of the Sawatch Mountain Range.

Begin skiing east up Chaffee Road 295. The road curves to the southeast and after 2.2 miles keep left and ascending at a fork. (The right fork descends to mine ruins at the former town site of Romley.) Chrysolite Mountain lies above to the south southeast. After crossing a bridge and passing an abandoned mine on your left, you will arrive at a sign and another fork at the terminus of this tour in 1.0 miles from the previous fork. The left road leads to the Pomeroy Lakes and the road to the right continues up to the ghost town of Hancock in 2.5 miles. For the return, the more adventurous skier may choose to descend steeply west and then north across Chalk Creek to the road back to Saint Elmo. I recommend the easy glide back on your ascent route.

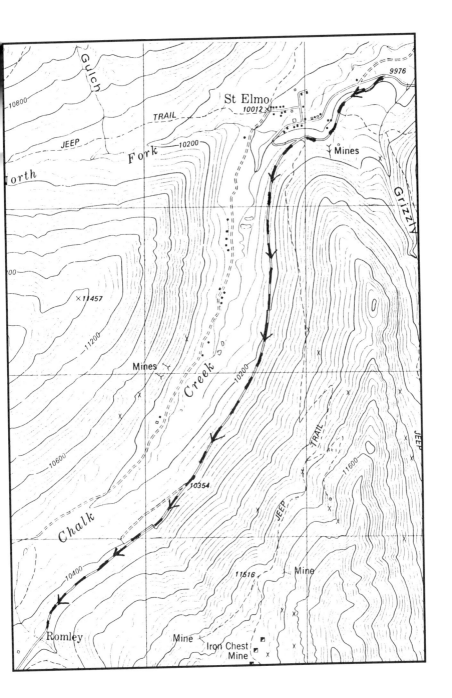

10B McCullough Gulch

Tour Distance:	2.9 miles each way
Tour Time:	Up in 77 minutes. Down in 66 minutes.
Starting Elevation:	10,848 feet
Highest Elevation:	11,350 feet (3459 meters)
Elevation Gain:	662 feet (inlcudes an extra 80 feet each way)
Avalanche Danger:	Moderate
Difficulty:	More Difficult
Steepness Index:	0.04
Trail:	All the way
Relevant Maps:	Breckenridge 7½ minute
	Trails Illustrated Number 109
	Summit County Number Two
	Arapaho National Forest

Getting There: From the traffic light in Breckenridge at Ski Hill Road drive south on Colorado 9 for 7.9 miles and turn right onto Summit County Road 850. After 1.0 miles on this road, which is also known as the Blue Lakes Road, you will reach an intersection with Summit County Road 851 on the right. Park here on the right at the beginning of Road 851 which is not ploughed.

This nordic ski outing takes you up McCullough Gulch, south of Breckenridge, to an old cabin. On a clear day the surrounding high peaks make this an especially beautiful ski tour.

Begin north on Road 851 and gradually ascend the gulch in a counterclockwise direction. The trail eventually descends past a green utility shed on your left. Take a left fork after 1.7 miles from the trailhead and stay high in the gulch. After 0.7 miles from the fork, the trail curves left (south) and becomes steeper as it passes around a road barrier and in a half mile after crossing a log bridge, reaches an old cabin. This is the terminus of this ski tour and a good spot for some rest and refreshment. The road continues to ascend to the right of the cabin farther up McCullough Gulch if you want to lengthen the tour. From the cabin Quandary Peak looms above to the southwest and Pacific Peak to the west northwest. Retrace your ascent route to return to your vehicle at the trailhead.

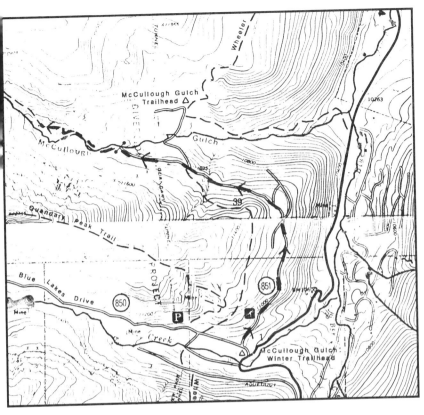

Courtesy of Trails Illustrated

11A Hunkidori Mine

Tour Distance: 3.6 miles each way
Tour Time: Up in 73 minutes. Down in 68 minutes.
Starting Elevation: 10,300 feet
Highest Elevation: 10,990 feet (3350 meters)
Elevation Gain: 1,010 feet (includes an extra 160 feet each way)
Avalanche Danger: Moderate
Difficulty: More Difficult
Steepness Index: 0.05
Trail: All the way
Relevant Maps: Montezuma 7½ minute
                     Keystone 7½ minute
                     Trails Illustrated Number 104
                     Trails Illustrated Cross-Country Skier's Map Number 401
                     Summit County Number Two
                     Arapaho National Forest (Dillon Ranger District)

Getting There: Drive on U.S. 6 either 8.5 miles south from Loveland Pass or 7.7 miles east from Exit 205 of Interstate 70 at Silverthorne and turn south onto the road to the Keystone Ski Area. Make the first possible left turn onto the Montezuma Road and follow it for 5.7 miles into the town of Montezuma and park on the right as Summit County Road 275 begins to descend toward Saints John.

47

Imagine a backcountry ski tour with beautiful scenery, lots of moderate down-hill runs with relatively low usage and a clear destination not too far from the trailhead. This close-to-perfect tour conforms to the route to the abandoned Hunkidori Mine. Most people who park at the trailhead follow the road up to Saints John and beyond but this alternate trip is special.

Start off by descending southwest to cross the Snake River and then ascending south southwest. Keep right and on the main road at a fork after 0.2 miles and after a half mile from the trailhead, reach the mouth of the Saints John Creek Valley. Take a right fork here off the main road, descend slightly and pass to the right of a wooden mine remnant and ascend northwest on a narrow road up into the trees. There follows a series of ups and downs as the old road curves in a counterclockwise fashion to enter Grizzly Gulch, ascends past an abandoned red truck and a cabin to reach the old Hunkidori Mine at the bottom of a steep bowl. Watch out for avalanches around here. The return has many delightful downhill runs, interspersed with some ascending terrain and there are even some nice views down into the Snake River Valley.

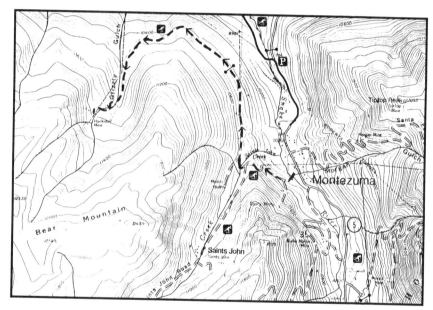

Courtesy of Trails Illustrated

11B West St. Louis Creek Trail

Tour Distance:	4.7 miles each way
Tour Time:	Up in 163 minutes. Down in 84 minutes
Starting Elevation:	9,055 feet
Highest Elevation:	10,560 feet (3219 meters)
Elevation Gain:	1,555 feet (includes an extra 25 feet each way)
Avalanche Danger:	Least
Difficulty:	More difficult
Steepness Index:	0.06
Trail:	All the way

48

Relevant Maps: Fraser 7½ minute
                   Bottle Pass 7½ minute
                   Grand County Number Four
                   Arapaho National Forest
                   Trails Illustrated Number 103

Getting There: On U.S. 40 drive north from the traffic light in Fraser for 0.2 miles and turn left onto Eisenhower Drive. Cross the train tracks and take an immediate left; turn onto Leonard Lane. After 0.2 miles from U.S. 40, turn right onto Mill Avenue and follow it straight up the valley. Pass the Fraser Experimental Forest sign and keep right at 2.8 miles from U.S. 40. Reach a 4-way intersection after 4.7 miles and take the right turn and park after 0.1 mile farther at a trailhead sign next to a log building.

This tour provides a gradual lengthy ascent on an old mining road to the beginning of the summer trail to Byers Peak. The sign at the parking area lists 3 different tours and this is the shortest and easiest.

The trail begins on the left side of the trail sign and the old log building. Ascend to the west southwest and stay on the road at all times. Keep left after 500 feet and take the right fork and head southwest 60 yards later. In another quarter mile take the left fork and continue to ascend through the woods to the south southwest. Eventually cross the creek and after 1.6 miles from the trailhead, keep right at a fork and continue the gradual ascent to the west. In 0.3 more miles take another right fork and continue west. (The left fork crosses the creek and will connect later with the main trail.) The road forks again in 0.7 miles and you should take the sharp right turn and proceed more steeply to the north. In 0.2 miles take a left fork and head south. In 1.5 more miles you will pass a Bottle Pass Trail sign on your right and 0.4 miles later, you will arrive at the road end at a sign for the Byers Peak Trail. Turn around here and enjoy the gentle descent with much double poling back to your vehicle at the trailhead.

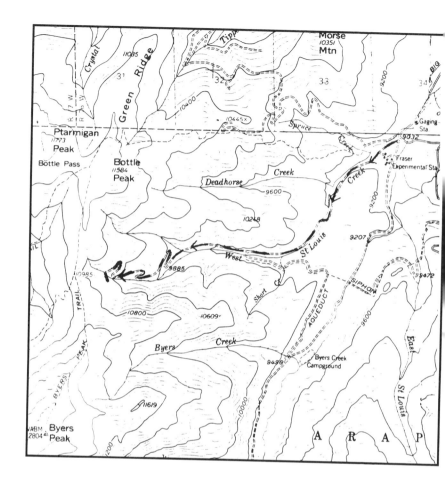

12A Mayflower Gulch

Tour Distance:	2.3 miles each way
Tour Time:	Up in 48 minutes. Down in 21 minutes.
Starting Elevation:	10,540 feet
Highest Elevation:	11,560 feet (3523 meters)
Elevation Gain:	1090 feet (includes 35 extra feet each way)
Avalanche Danger:	Moderate (at higher levels)
Difficulty:	More Difficult
Steepness Index:	0.09
Trail:	All the way
Relevant Maps:	Copper Mountain 7½ minute
	Trails Illustrated Number 109
	Trails Illustrated Cross-Country Skier's Map Number 401
	Summit County Number Two
	Arapaho National Forest (Dillon Ranger District)

Getting There: From Exit 195 off Interstate 70 at Copper Mountain, drive south on Colorado 91 for 6.1 miles. Then turn left onto an open area and park near a sign stating "Public Access Road."

The snow at this time of year can be rather icy and we may be into the last weeks of nordic skiing for the season. However, Mayflower Gulch provides a beautiful ski tour into an open basin with some abandoned cabins on the northwestern slopes of Fletcher Mountain. The high mountain scenery is great throughout the tour.

Begin east southeast up the road and take the right fork after a few hundred yards. Follow the road with some fairly steep portions and arrive into a large open basin with a few abandoned cabins, which were associated with the former Boston Mine, in 2.3 miles from the trailhead. Mayflower Hill lies to the north northeast and Jaque Peak is prominent far down the gulch to the west northwest. These cabins are the destination for this tour but you may want to explore the area further or free ski in the open basin. There are wonderful downhill runs on the wide road back to your vehicle.

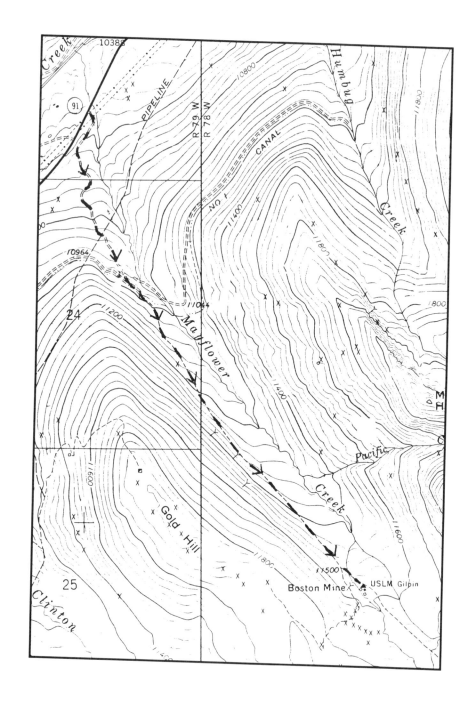

12B Zimmerman Lake Loop Trail

Tour Distance:	3.1 miles total loop
Tour Time:	Total loop in 78 minutes
Starting Elevation:	10,010 feet
Highest Elevation:	10,560 feet (3219 meters)
Elevation Gain:	665 feet (includes 115 extra feet)
Avalanche Danger:	Least
Difficulty:	More difficult
Steepness Index:	0.08
Trail:	All the way
Relevant Maps:	Clark Peak 7½ minute
	Chambers Lake 7½ minute
	Trails Illustrated Number 112
	Larimer County Number Three
	Roosevelt National Forest

Getting There: From U.S. 287 northwest of Fort Collins, drive west on Colorado 14 up Poudre Canyon for 56.3 miles and park in the designated area on the left. (This area lies 1.5 miles before Cameron Pass is reached.)

This loop trail around Zimmerman Lake provides some good downhill areas and is best done clockwise. There is usually good snow in this area from December through March.

Begin your tour by going east southeast from the trailhead building off the parking area. There are some helpful maps on the front wall of this structure. Follow the road and the blue diamond markers. The route soon curves left and ascends more steeply. In 1.1 miles from the trailhead reach a sign and take the left fork toward Zimmerman Lake. In 0.2 more miles you will ascend to another sign and a fork. The right fork goes to the lake. Take the left fork, leave the road and follow the good trail markers through the woods. Continue to ascend above the lake before the trail takes a sharp right turn to return close to the edge of the lake. The trail will eventually reach an open area which descends to reach the earlier reached fork and sign. Go left and enjoy the rapid, downhill glide back to the trailhead.

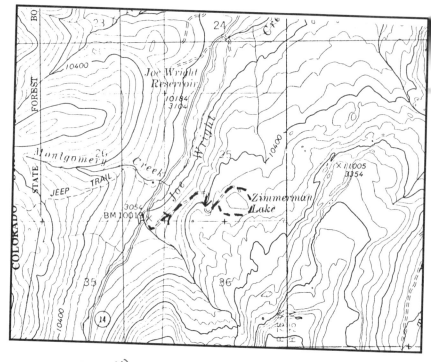

12/16/2000

13A French Gulch

Tour Distance: 3.1 miles each way
Tour Time: Up in 77 minutes. Down in 52 minutes.
Starting Elevation: 10,280 feet
Highest Elevation: 10,880 feet (3316 meters)
Elevation Gain: 960 feet (includes an extra 180 feet each way)
Avalanche Danger: Significant
Difficulty: Easiest
Steepness Index: 0.06
Trail: All the way
Relevant Maps: Boreas Pass 7½ minute
                      Trails Illustrated Number 109
                      Trails Illustrated Cross-Country Skier's Map Number 401
                      Summit County Number Three
                      Arapaho National Forest

Getting There: On Colorado 9, drive south from Main Street in Frisco for 8.5 miles and turn left onto Summit County Road 450. (This turnoff is 0.3 miles north of the Breckenridge town boundary.) Follow Road 450 and take a right fork after 0.35 miles from Colorado 9 and pass through a group of homes. After 0.7 miles farther, go left onto Summit County Road 2 and continue past remnants of old mining up into French Gulch. After 2.8 miles on Road 2, park off the right side of the road. Summit County maintains the road up to this point.

French Gulch is the valley just north of the Boreas Pass Road and provides a gentle ascent between Mount Guyot on the left and Bald Mountain on the right. The scenery is gorgeous, the snow is usually abundant and there are some open areas for free skiing at the upper levels.

From the parking area head east along the wide road. Avoid the immediate left fork to Humbug Hill and the right fork a few hundred yards down the road and stay on the main trail which leads southeast and south up French Gulch. You will pass a road barrier which may be open and in 1.1 miles from the trailhead, pass the cutoff to the left leading up Little French Gulch. Ski tour by a small clearing and some houses and in another half hour reach the beginning of a large clearing. Continue up the gulch on the left side of the creek. You will traverse this clearing in less than a quarter hour. At the far southern edge of the clearing is the terminus of this tour. There are two options if you wish to go farther. The first is to follow the road southeast into the trees past a road barrier and up to French Pass. The second option is to bear right and quickly cross the creek and turn left (south) to enter a small clearing where some free skiing is possible.

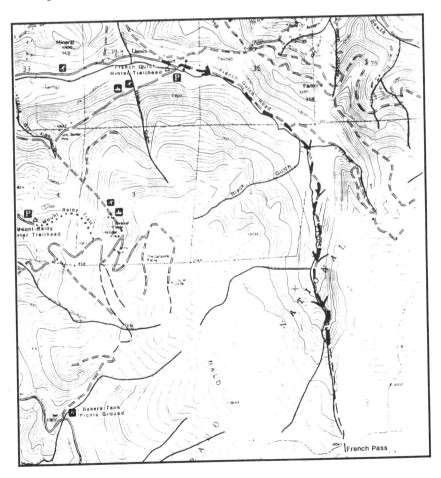

Courtesy of Trails Illustrated

13B Keystone Gulch

Tour Distance:	3.3 miles total loop
Tour Time:	Up in 86 minutes. Down in 52 minutes.
Starting Elevation:	9,265 feet
Highest Elevation:	10,080 feet (3072 meters)
Elevation Gain:	827 feet (includes 12 extra feet)
Avalanche Danger:	Least
Difficulty:	Easiest
Steepness Index:	0.05
Trail:	All the way
Relevant Maps:	Keystone 7½ minute
	Trails Illustrated Number 104
	Summit County Number Two
	Arapaho National Forest (Dillon Ranger District)

Getting There: From Exit 205 of Interstate 70 at Silverthorne, drive south on U.S. 6 for 5.5 miles and turn right at the stoplight into the Keystone Resort complex. Make a quick left turn and then make your first possible right turn after 0.3 miles from U.S. 6 onto Soda Ridge Road. Drive on Soda Ridge Road for 0.5 miles to the Keystone Gulch Road which will be on your left. Turn left and drive up this road for a tenth of a mile and park along the side of the road just before the road barrier.

This cross county ski route ascends the well-plowed Keystone Gulch Road and ends at one of the Keystone downhill ski lifts in a back bowl. This tour avoids contact with the main Keystone downhill operation which lies a mile to the east.

Begin southeast up the Keystone Gulch Road which is closed to automobiles. You will pass around a metal barrier which blocks the road. Continue the gradual ascent southeast and after several creek crossings you will first pass a large metal building and then the ski lift on your left in about 3.3 miles from the trailhead. At this point, which is the destination of this description, the road forks. (The left fork ascends to the alpine runs and lift area. The right fork continues southeast up the gulch another 1.3 miles to a North Peak lift which starts on the right and passes over the road. The road above this lift experiences lots of downhill skier traffic.) The descent is gradual with considerable double poling and a few easy runs.

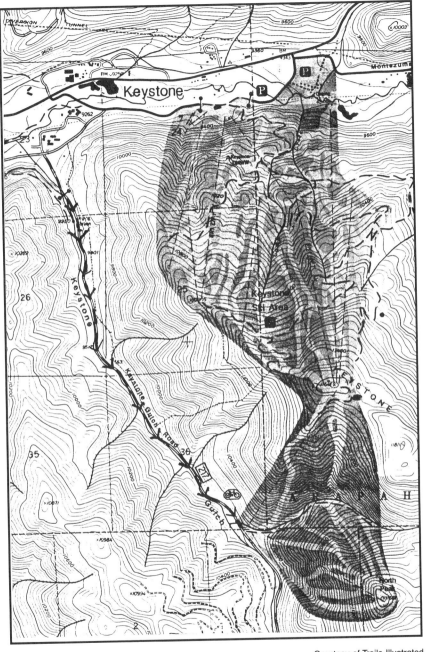

Courtesy of Trails Illustrated

14A   Green Mountain (City of Lakewood)

Hike Distance: 1.5 miles each way
Hiking Time: Up in 33 minutes. Down in 28 minutes.
Starting Elevation: 6,050 feet
Highest Elevation: 6,855 feet (2089 meters)
Elevation Gain: 805 feet
Difficulty: Easy
Steepness Index: 0.10
Trail: All the way until last 150 feet
Relevant Maps: Morrison 7½ minute
                        Jefferson County Number One
                        Green Mountain Park (City of Lakewood)
Views from the Summit: NE to Denver
                        NW to Lookout Mountain, Chiefs Head Peak,
                        Pagoda Mountain, Longs Peak and Mount Meeker
                        SSE to Pikes Peak and Long Scraggy Peak
                        SW to Mount Morrison, Meridian Hill and Mount
                        Evans
                        W to Chief Mountain
                        WNW to James Peak
                        WSW to Squaw Mountain

Getting There: From the junction of Interstate 70 and U.S. 6 in Lakewood, drive west on U.S. 6 for 0.6 miles and turn left onto U.S. 40 west. Follow U.S. 40 west for 0.5 miles and turn left onto Rooney Road. Follow Rooney Road on a bridge over I-70 for a total of 1.9 miles to the south and turn left into a paved parking area which is provided by the City of Lakewood for Green Mountain Park.

Green Mountain, just west of Denver, is a City of Lakewood Park and the shorter of two mountains with the same name in Jefferson County. It provides the closest mountain view of Denver. Its easy accessibility makes it a possible outing after work or over a long lunch hour. This is one of several trailheads for Green Mountain and has the best parking area and the shortest distance to the top.

Begin the hike to the southeast from the parking area on a paved trail which crosses a bridge over Colorado 470. Pass the intersection with a bike path and continue east onto a gravel road which initially curves north but generally leads east up through grassy slopes to a ridge and a fork. Turn right and ascend southeast for about 5 minutes and then go right (south southwest) off the road for the last 150 feet to the treeless, high point which is marked only by a few rock piles. If it's a clear day, take in all the views and you may want to explore the summit mesa and its many trails before retracing your ascent route back to the trailhead.

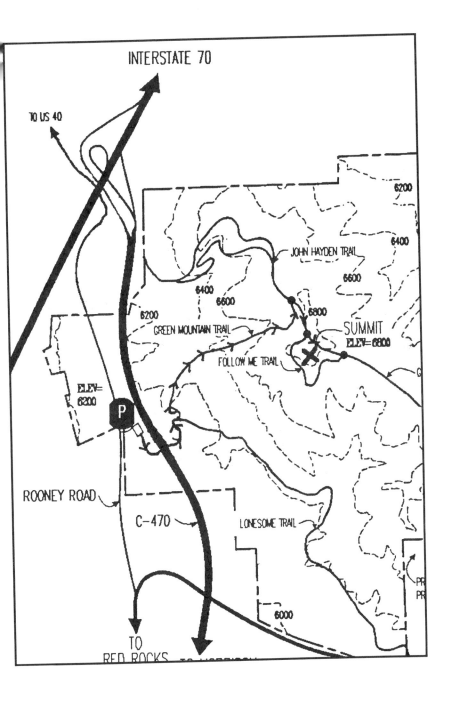

INTERSTATE 70

TO US 40

6200

6400

JOHN HAYDEN TRAIL

6600

6400

6600

6800

6200

GREEN MOUNTAIN TRAIL

SUMMIT
ELEV=6800

FOLLOW ME TRAIL

ELEV=
6200

P

ROONEY ROAD

C-470

LONESOME TRAIL

PR
PR

6000

TO
RED ROCKS

59

14B Mount Sanitas

Hike Distance:	1.3 miles each way
Hiking Time:	Up in 43 minutes. Down in 36 minutes.
Starting Elevation:	5,510 feet
Highest Elevation:	6,863 feet (2092 meters)
Elevation Gain:	1,383 feet (includes 15 extra feet each way)
Difficulty:	Easy
Steepness Index:	0.21
Trail:	All the way
Relevant Maps:	Boulder 7½ minute
	Boulder County
	Roosevelt National Forest
	City of Boulder Open Space Trail Map
Views from the Summit:	E to Boulder
	SSE to Green Mountain
	WNW to Chiefs Head Peak and Mount Meeker
	WSW to James Peak

Getting There: From Broadway in central Boulder, drive west on Mapleton Avenue for 0.8 miles and park just past Boulder Memorial Hospital on the right at a trailhead sign. (This road continues northwest up Sunshine Canyon as Boulder Road 52.)

Mount Sanitas can be hiked virtually the entire year. It will be free of snow generally from March into November. This mountain trail is part of the free, well-marked and maintained Boulder Open Space which includes the Mesa Trail and the trails to Green Mountain, Bear Peak and South Boulder Peak. Sanitas is an unofficial name commemorating the nearby former sanitarium which became Boulder Memorial Hospital.

For the hike descend slightly from the parking area and pass through a semi-open red brick structure and cross a small creek. Then take a left fork and ascend steeply to the northwest. The trail is often steep as it proceeds along the spine of the mountain. Eventually you pass northwest under some power lines to reach several large rocks with an embedded metal pole at the summit. The view of Boulder to the east is memorable. Trees partially block the views to the west.

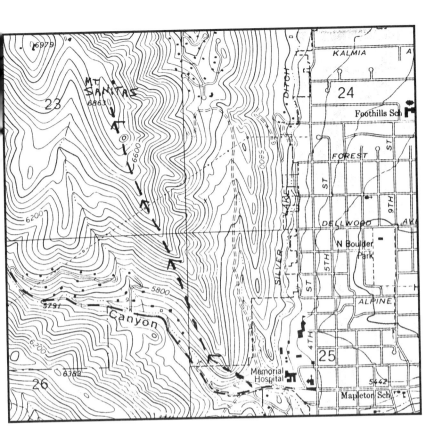

15A Arthurs Rock

Hike Distance:	1.7 miles each way
Hiking Time:	Up in 53 minutes. Down in 42 minutes.
Starting Elevation:	5,620 feet
Highest Elevation:	6,780 feet (2067 meters)
Elevation Gain:	1,210 feet (includes an extra 25 feet each way)
Difficulty:	Easy
Steepness Index:	0.13
Trail:	All the way
Relevant Maps:	Horsetooth Reservoir 7½ minute
	Larimer County Number Four
	Roosevelt National Forest
	Lory State Park Open Space Trail Map
Views from the Summit:	NE to SE to Horsetooth Reservoir
	E to Fort Collins
	S to Horsetooth Rock

Getting There: Drive northwest of Fort Collins via U.S. 287 to the towns of Laporte and Bellvue and then follow the signs about 3 miles south to the entrance of Lory State Park. Pay the admission fee and drive south on the gravel road for 2.2 miles to the end of the road at the Arthurs Rock Trailhead and park.

Lory State Park is named after Charles A. Lory who was the President of Colorado State University from 1909 until 1940. The park lies along the western shore of Horsetooth Reservoir and offers 30 miles of hiking trails, picnic facilities, some horseback trails and even some backcountry camp sites. Park history identifies a local settler, named Arthur, who frequently climbed in this area. This could make a special family outing with the wide variety of available activities.

Begin on the clear trail from the sign and trail register. Wind up a narrow canyon along a creek. Keep left at the first trail intersection and sign. Arthurs Rock now becomes visible as you ascend the gulch to the northwest. Keep right at the next two forks, then left at a four-way intersection near an overlook and finally right just before your final approach. After the last fork, approach the rock and then descend about 15 feet along its western side and then just past a sign, ascend a rocky gully to your left and reach a saddle over-looking Horsetooth Reservoir. Turn left at the saddle and cross bare rock to the high point just past a solitary tree. Be careful on this rock since a misstep could prove very harmful. Children should definitely be supervised on this final segment. Enjoy the wonderful scenery and retrace your ascent route unless you would like to take the longer Timber Trail or the shorter Overlook Trail (CF Lory State Park Map) back to the trailhead.

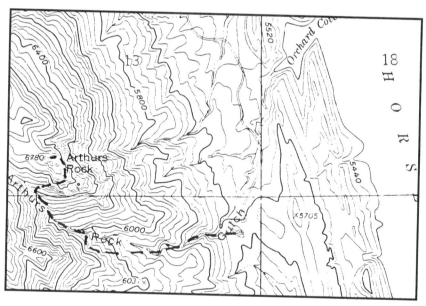

15B Reynolds Park – Eagles View

Hike Distance:	2.9 miles (total loop)
Hiking Time:	Up in 60 minutes. Down in 40 minutes.
Starting Elevation:	7,290 feet
Highest Elevation:	8,140 feet (2481 meters)
Elevation Gain:	1,010 feet (includes 160 extra feet)
Difficulty:	Easy
Steepness Index:	0.13
Trail:	All the way
Relevant Maps:	Platte Canyon 7½ minute
	Pine 7½ minute
	Jefferson County Number Two
	Reynolds Park (Jefferson County Open Space)
Views from the Summit:	S to the Cathedral Spires
	SSE to Pikes Peak
	SSW to Green Mountain
	SE to Long Scraggy Peak

Getting There: Drive southwest on U.S. 285 for 0.5 miles from the stop light in Conifer and turn left onto Foxton Road (Jefferson County Number 97). Drive 5.1 miles from U.S. 285 and park on the right in the designated area for Reynolds Park.

This is an early season loop hike in one of the fine, convenient Jefferson County parks. No fee is required and with picnic tables, a toilet and an interpretive trail, this is a great park for a family outing. Pets must be kept on a leash.

Begin hiking by descending slightly to the trailhead and continue to the south southwest up to a four-way intersection and a toilet facility on your right. Take the right fork and in about fifty feet take another right fork. After 0.2 more miles keep straight (west) at another four-way intersection on the Raven's Roost Trail. After 0.6 miles take a left fork and descend 0.3 miles to a fork. Go right and ascend the Eagles View Trail to the south southeast. Reach a ridge and continue up to a park boundary sign. This is the Eagles View and the end of this hike. There are good views to the south. Return back 0.7 miles on the Eagles View Trail to the fork which you left earlier. This time turn right and descend the Oxen Draw Trail. After 0.6 miles take a right fork followed by a very quick left fork. In about one hundred yards reach another fork and go right and reach the initial four-way intersection and continue left down to your vehicle.

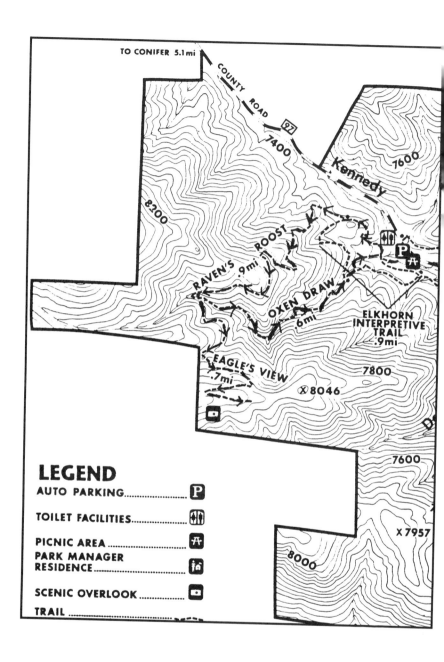

TO CONIFER 5.1mi

COUNTY ROAD

97

7400

Kennedy

7600

8200

RAVEN'S ROOST .9mi

OXEN DRAW .6mi

ELKHORN INTERPRETIVE TRAIL .9mi

7800

EAGLE'S VIEW .7mi

X 8046

7600

X 7957

8000

LEGEND

AUTO PARKING...................... **P**

TOILET FACILITIES...................

PICNIC AREA ....

PARK MANAGER
RESIDENCE...............................

SCENIC OVERLOOK ....

TRAIL ....

16A Greyrock Mountain

Hike Distance: 3.2 miles each way
Hiking Time: Up in 114 minutes. Down in 104 minutes.
Starting Elevation: 5,558 feet
Highest Elevation: 7,613 feet (2320 meters)
Elevation Gain: 2,295 feet (includes an extra 120 feet each way due to
                     undulations in the trail)
Difficulty: Moderate
Steepness Index: 0.14
Trail: All the way
Relevant Maps: Poudre Park 7½ minute
                     Larimer County Number Two
                     Roosevelt National Forest
Views from the Summit: ESE to Fort Collins
                     SSE to Horsetooth Rock
                     SE to Horsetooth Reservoir
                     SW to Mount Dickinson and the Mummy Range

Getting There: From northwest of Fort Collins on U.S. 287, drive west on
Colorado 14 for 8.1 miles and park on the left in the designated area.

For this early in the hiking season, a good hike will be on a south facing
slope with not too much elevation and in an area which doesn't receive a
large snowfall. The Greyrock Mountain Trail meets all these specifications
and provides some enjoyable, easy rock scrambling near the top.

From the west end of the parking area descend some stairs to the northwest,
cross Colorado 14 and descend farther to a wooden bridge over the Cache
La Poudre River. The trail then turns west and in 0.7 miles from the trailhead
you will reach a fork and a sign. Take the right fork (north) to Greyrock
Mountain. The left fork leads to Greyrock Meadows. Gradually ascend a
small canyon and in about 1.2 miles from the fork, huge Greyrock Mountain
comes into view. After 0.2 more miles you will reach a second fork. Keep
straight since the left fork leads back to Greyrock Meadows. The trail descends some as you ascend Greyrock in a counterclockwise fashion. Carefully
follow a series of cairns and about halfway up at a large rock with a cairn,
continue to your right. Eventually rise west southwest to a flat open area just
below the summit (which is visible to the south southwest). Proceed southwest
through some trees and then over the rocks past a large pond on your right.
Some easy hand work will be necessary to reach the rocky unmarked top
but there is no special danger. Take in the great views and then carefully
retrace your ascent route beginning to the north northeast.

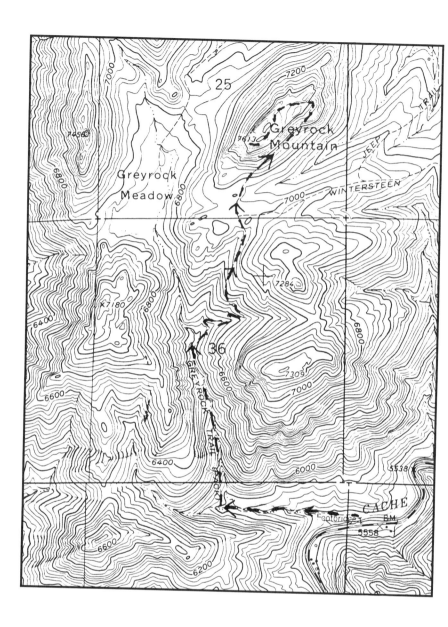

16B Mount McConnel

Hike Distance:	2.2 miles on the ascent. 2.7 miles on the descent. (loop)
Hiking Time:	Up in 63 minutes. Down in 61 minutes.
Starting Elevation:	6,610 feet
Highest Elevation:	8,010 feet (2441 meters)
Elevation Gain:	1,590 feet (includes an extra 190 feet of elevation gain due to undulations in the trail)
Difficulty:	Moderate
Steepness Index:	0.14
Trail:	All the way
Relevant Maps:	Big Narrows 7½ minute
	Larimer County Number Two
	Roosevelt National Forest
Views from the Summit:	SSE to West White Pine Mountain
	SW to the Mummy Range
	WNW to South, Middle and North Bald Mountains
	WSW to South and North Rawah Peaks

Getting There: From U.S. 287 northwest of Fort Collins, drive west on Colorado 14 through lovely Poudre Canyon for 23.8 miles to a Roosevelt National Forest sign on the left and a bridge crossing the Cache la Poudre River. The road over this bridge is blocked to vehicular traffic both early and late in the hiking season. Park around here.

Mount McConnel is a good early or late season hike and should now be free of snow. The Kreutzer Nature Trail, named after the first national forest ranger, overlaps part of the route and provides a series of informational signs along the way.

To begin the hike, cross the bridge and stay on the road going south southwest. Take the left fork and pass the Mountain Park Campground on your right en route to a trailhead sign on your left. Proceed up and east northeast on the trail which rises in 1.2 miles (from the bridge) to a fork. Take the right fork, which is the summit trail, to the southwest. Eventually pass a wilderness sign and shortly before the top take a right fork at a trail sign and 0.2 miles later reach the unmarked summit on a boulder amid a few trees. Some easy hand work will be needed here. After taking in the views to the south and west, retrace your ascent route for one mile to a fork and go right (southeast), onto the nature trail which weaves downward, steeply at times, with many switchbacks to another fork which is reached in 2.1 miles from the summit. Take the left fork and descend northwest to reach the end of the trail at the south end of the bridge from where you began. After your hike, check your body and clothes for ticks since they are abundant in April and May.

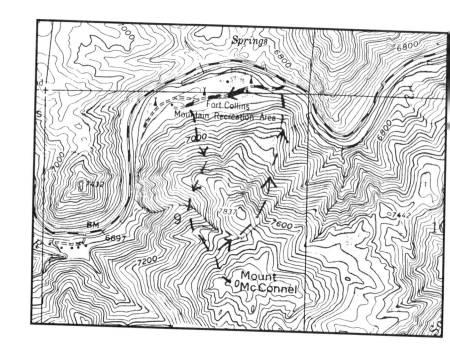

17A Bridal Veil Falls

Hike Distance:	3.4 miles each way
Hiking Time:	Up in 79 minutes. Down in 73 minutes.
Starting Elevation:	7,830 feet
Highest Elevation:	8,720 feet (2658 meters)
Elevation Gain:	1,030 feet (includes 65 feet extra each way)
Difficulty:	Easy
Steepness Index:	0.06
Trail:	All the way
Relevant Maps:	Estes Park 7½ minute
	Trails Illustrated Number 200
	Larimer County Number Four
	Roosevelt National Forest
	Rocky Mountain National Park

Getting There: From Drake on U.S. 34, take the road northwest through Glen Haven. After 11.4 miles from Drake, turn right onto the good dirt road to McGraw Ranch. Don't be discouraged by the signs since this road will lead to the trailhead and Rocky Mountain National Park. This road can also be reached from the junction of U.S. 34 and U.S. 36 in Estes Park by driving west on U.S. 34 for 0.5 miles and turning right onto the MacGregor Ranch Road which becomes the Devils Gulch Road. The McGraw Ranch Road will be 6.0 miles from the U.S. 36 and U.S. 34 intersection in Estes Park. Drive on the good dirt road toward McGraw Ranch. Keep straight at 1.0 miles, left at 1.1 miles and park at 2.1 miles, off the road, just before crossing a bridge to the former McGraw Ranch.

This hike to Bridal Veil Falls utilizes the excellent trail system of Rocky Mountain National Park and yet no park fee is required. Pets and vehicles are forbidden. The trail is gradual and steepens just before you reach the lovely waterfall. Spring is a good time for this hike since the snowmelt provides good drainage into Cow Creek. Numerous beaver dams can be seen on the creek.

Cross the bridge over Cow Creek on foot and pass to the right of a trailhead sign board on the clear trail through the buildings of the former McGraw Ranch. Follow the trail as it turns to the left and runs parallel to Cow Creek on the left. After just 200 yards from the trailhead keep left at a fork and stay on the Cow Creek Trail. After one mile take a right fork and continue southwest up the valley. (The left fork goes to Gem Lake.) Pass Rabbit Ears Campsite on your left and in 0.8 miles more take the right fork at a sign. (The left fork is the Black Canyon Trail.) You will make 3 creek crossings and in 1.2 miles from the last fork you reach a corral and sign. Ascend the trail more steeply and in 0.3 miles from the corral the trail ends at the foot of photogenic Bridal Veil Falls. Enjoy the falls and the mist before retracing your route back.

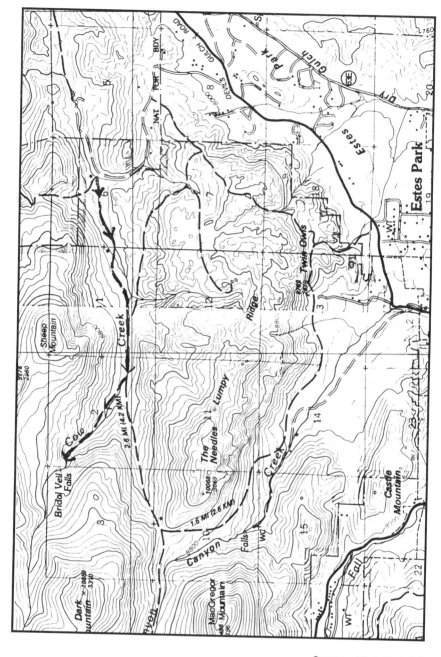

Courtesy of Trails Illustrated

17B Carpenter Peak

Hike Distance:	2.7 miles each way
Hiking Time:	Up in 72 minutes. Down in 68 minutes.
Starting Elevation:	6,200 feet
Highest Elevation:	7,205 feet
Elevation Gain:	1,185 feet (includes 90 feet of extra elevation gain each way)
Difficulty:	Easy
Steepness Index:	0.08
Trail:	All the way
Relevant Maps:	Kassler 7½ minute
	Douglas County Number One
	Roxborough State Park
	Pike National Forrest
Views from the summit:	N to Chatfield Reservoir and Denver
	ENE to Roxborough Park Visitor Center
	SE to Pikes Peak
	SW to Long Scraggy Peak
	WNW to Rosalie Peak

Getting There: Drive south on U.S. 85 from its juncture with Colorado 470 for 4.4 miles and turn right (west) on Titan Road. Follow Titan Road which becomes Douglas County Road 7 and then Douglas County Road 5 for 7.0 miles as it curves southwest. Then turn left onto a dirt road which is Douglas County Road 3. After 100 yards, turn right and follow this road for 2.2 miles into Roxborough State Park to the parking area near the visitor center. Or from Colorado 470 drive south on Wadsworth Avenue (Colorado 121) for 2.2 miles and turn left onto Waterton Road and follow it for 1.6 miles to a T. Turn right onto Titan Road for 2.3 more miles and then turn left and follow the signs to Roxborough Park for 2.3 miles.

Roxborough was the name of the Irish family estate of Henry Persse. He and Julius Carpenter were homesteaders in this area. Roxborough State Park charges an entry fee and pets are forbidden. The surrounding red rock formations are impressive.

Begin on the Carpenter Peak Trail which leads southwest from the visitor center. After 0.3 miles take the right fork at a sign and continue southeast and later southwest. In two hundred yards take a second right fork. The trail crosses a dirt road, goes up and down often and has many switchbacks as it reaches a bluff and then descends into a gulch before the final ascent which proceeds north northwest to the rocky unmarked summit. A left fork near the top reaches the Colorado Trail in 4.5 miles. Descend as you came up on the trail.

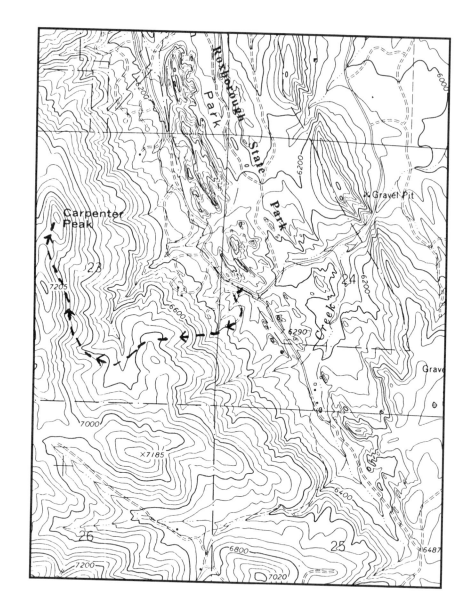

18A West Creek Falls

Hike Distance:	2.8 miles each way
Hiking Time:	Up in 69 minutes. Down in 59 minutes.
Starting Elevation:	7,830 feet
Highest Elevation:	8,460 feet (2579 meters)
Elevation Gain:	1,520 feet (due to trail undulations)
Difficulty:	Moderate
Steepness Index:	0.10
Trail:	All the way

72

Relevant Maps: Estes Park 7½ minute
                  Larimer County Number Four
                  Roosevelt National Forest
                  Rocky Mountain National Park
                  Trails Illustrated Number 200

Getting There: From the junction of U.S. 36 and U.S. 34 in Estes Park, drive west on U.S. 34 for 0.4 miles and turn right onto MacGregor Avenue and follow it as it becomes the Devils Gulch Road for 5.6 miles from U.S. 34. Then leave the paved road and turn left onto the McGraw Ranch Road. Stay on the main road and keep left at mile 1.1 and right at mile 1.4 from the Devils Gulch Road. Enter Rocky Mountain National Park and park at mile 2.2 just before the road ends at the old McGraw Ranch.

The West Creek Falls hike begins at the old McGraw Ranch, uses the North Boundary Trail and ends up within Rocky Mountain National Park. The area receives relatively little snowfall and this route should be open from April through November.

Start your hike by crossing Cow Creek on a bridge and ascending north northwest into the former McGraw Ranch. The trail curves to the left and in about 300 yards take the right fork and ascend the North Boundary Trail. Pass a trail register and rise 0.7 miles to the highest point of this hike at 8,460 feet. Continue west and descend steeply about 500 feet to West Creek. Cross the creek on a log and go left at a T and a trail sign. After 0.3 miles farther take the left fork at another trail sign and continue 0.7 more miles on a faint trail on the northwest (right) side of the creek to the gentle falls of West Creek. Take some refreshment, rest and maybe some pictures before retracing your route back to the McGraw Ranch.

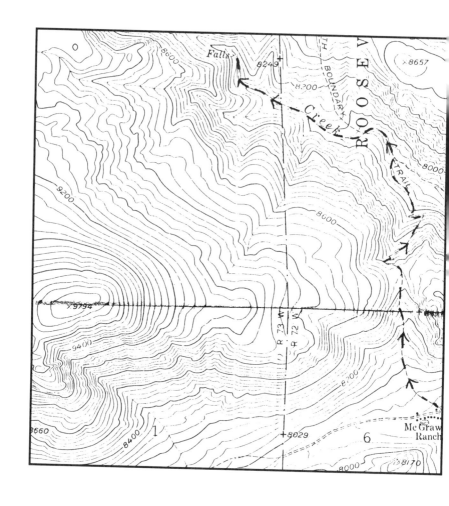

18B Green Mountain (Boulder County)

Hike Distance: 1.3 miles each way
Hiking Time: Up in 40 minutes. Down in 36 minutes.
Starting Elevation: 7,690 feet
Highest Elevation: 8,144 feet (2482 meters)
Elevation Gain: 714 feet (includes 130 feet of extra elevation gain each
                      way)
Difficulty: Easy
Steepness Index: 0.10
Trail: All the way
Relevant Maps: Eldorado Springs 7½ minute
                      Boulder County
                      Boulder Mountain Park Trail Map
Views from the Summit: NE to Boulder
                      NW to McHenrys Peak, Chiefs Head Peak, Pagoda
                      Mountain, Longs Peak, Mount Meeker, Estes Cone,
                      Ypsilon Mountain and Twin Sisters Peaks

SE to Bear Peak and South Boulder Peak
SW to Thorodin Mountain, Mount Bancroft, James
Peak, Mount Neva and South Arapaho Peak
WNW to Bald Mountain

Getting There: From Broadway in Boulder, drive west up Baesline Road past Flagstaff Mountain for 6.1 miles to a sign and the trailhead on the left. Park around this point off the road.

There are several Green Mountains in Colorado. This one overlooks Boulder from the west and is a popular hike. The route I will describe here is the easiest of several ways to the top and the summit views are impressive.

Begin southeast from your vehicle on the clearly marked Green Mountain West Ridge Trail. The trail descends and rises on occasion as you ascend the west ridge through the trees and steepens near the top. The summit lies amid large boulders and is marked by a stone column with a metal plate which states the directions and elevations of 24 peaks visible from this point. A register cylinder is encased within the column. Return by your ascent route.

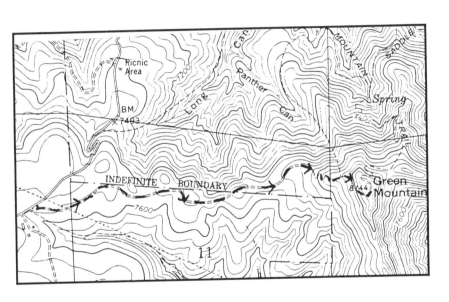

19A Royal Arch

Hike Distance:	1.8 miles each way
Hiking Time:	Up in 52 minutes. Down in 50 minutes.
Starting Elevation:	5,670 feet
Highest Elevation:	6,850 feet (2088 meters)
Elevation Gain:	1,412 feet (includes an extra 116 feet each way)
Difficulty:	Easy
Steepness Index:	0.15
Trail:	All the way

Relevant Maps: Eldorado Springs 7½ minute
Boulder County
Boulder Mountain Park Trail Map
Boulder Open Space Trails Map
Views from the Summit: NE to the University of Colorado (Boulder)
E to the National Center for Atmospheric Research

Getting There: From Broadway in Boulder, drive west up Baseline Road for 1.1 miles and turn left into Chautauqua Park and park in the lot to your right.

The hike to Royal Arch takes you near the impressive Boulder Flatirons. You may even see a technical climber negotiating one of their sheer walls. This good, steep, rocky trail is usually hikeable from April to November.

Start hiking to the south from the parking area and ascend a steep road which is closed to automobiles. After 0.4 miles you pass the Mesa Trail and a toilet facility on your left. Keep left at a fork and rise to the Bluebell Shelter. Just before the shelter the trail to Royal Arch descends to the left. In one tenth of a mile farther, keep left (south southwest) on the main trail as an unmarked trail ascends steeply to the right. As the trail continues its steep ascent, one of the "Flatirons" can be seen up and to your right. Eventually reach a ridge and then descend almost 100 feet before a final steep ascent to a rocky area just below Royal Arch. Take in the vistas to the north and east. Be sure to take two consecutive left forks in your return to the ridge.

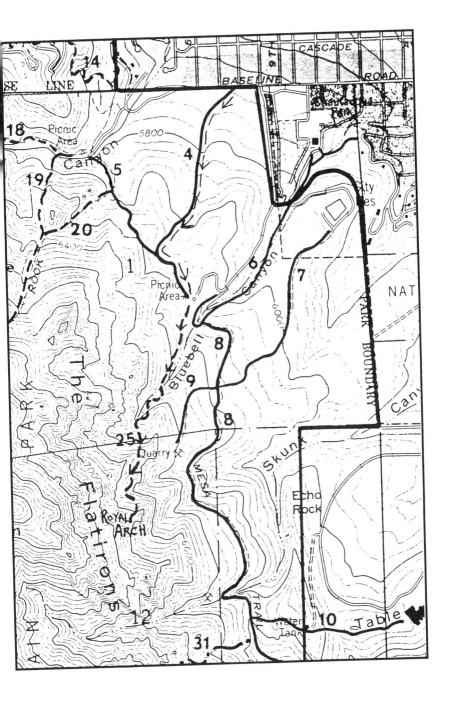

19B UTE TRAIL (ASPEN)

Hike Distance:	1.1 miles each way
Hiking Time:	Up in 40 minutes. Down in 35 minutes.
Starting Elevation:	7,990 feet
Highest Elevation:	9,200 feet (2804 meters)
Elevation Gain:	1,300 feet (includes 45 extra feet each way)
Difficulty:	Moderate
Steepness Index:	0.22
Trail:	All the way
Relevant Maps:	Aspen 7½ minute
	Trails Illustrated Number 127
	Pitkin County Number Two
	White River National Forest

Getting There: From the intersection at East Cooper Street in Aspen, drive south on South Original Street for two blocks to a T. Then turn left onto Ute Avenue and drive 0.4 miles farther. Park in the open area on the left with the sign for the Ute Trail on the right.

The Ute Trail in Aspen is very steep and heavily used. Some Aspenites ascend the trail daily to condition themselves. The view of Aspen from the rocky promontory at the high point of the trail is a generous reward for the hiker's persistence.

Start up the Ute Trail to the south from the trailhead sign. Keep on the clear main trail as it switchbacks steeply up through the bushes and trees. Within the initial 800 feet from the trailhead, take a left fork, a right fork and another left fork. Loose gravel can diminish your footing on the narrow parts of the trail. As you reach the several rocky ledges at trails end, a spur trail ascends through the trees to the south to connect with a gondola terminus on Aspen Mountain. Enjoy the great view north to Aspen and west to one of the twin summits of Mount Sopris. Be careful on the steep descent.

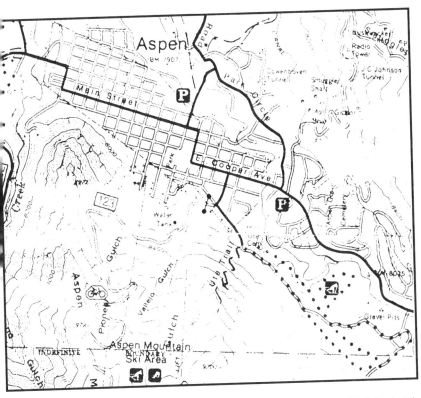

20A Green Mountain – Tonahutu Trail Loop

Hike Distance:	5.9 miles (total loop)
Hiking Time:	136 minutes (total loop)
Starting Elevation:	8,800 feet
Highest Elevation:	9,450 feet (2880 meters)
Elevation Gain:	828 feet (includes 178 extra feet)
Difficulty:	Easy
Steepness Index:	0.05
Trail:	All the way
Relevant Maps:	Grand Lake 7½ minute
	Trails Illustrated Number 200
	Grand County Number Two
	Rocky Mountain National Park

Getting There: Drive to the Kawuneeche Visitor Center in Rocky Mountain National Park on U.S. 36 northwest of Grand Lake and park one vehicle 100 yards south of the visitor center at the trailhead sign. Drive the second vehicle 2.9 miles farther north on U.S. 36 and park at the Green Mountain Trailhead. From here you will begin your hike.

This loop hike lies within Rocky Mountain National Park, requires two vehicles and can be done from May into November. It leads past Big Meadows, an extensive flat area with several intersecting trails. Nakai Peak can be seen

79

to the north northeast from Big Meadows. Tonahutu is an Arapaho Indian word meaning Big Meadows.

Start hiking to the east on the clear, well-signed trail. Rise through the trees and after reaching a ridge descend to a fork and trail signs after 1.5 miles from the trailhead. Take the right fork and after 0.3 miles reach Big Meadows. Continue south on the trail paralleling Tonahutu Creek on your left. The trail rises and falls gently for 3.6 miles to a fork and more trail signs. (En route to this point an old wooden conduit can be seen to the left of the trail.) Turn right at the fork and reach the trailhead at the Kawuneeche Visitor Center in another half mile.

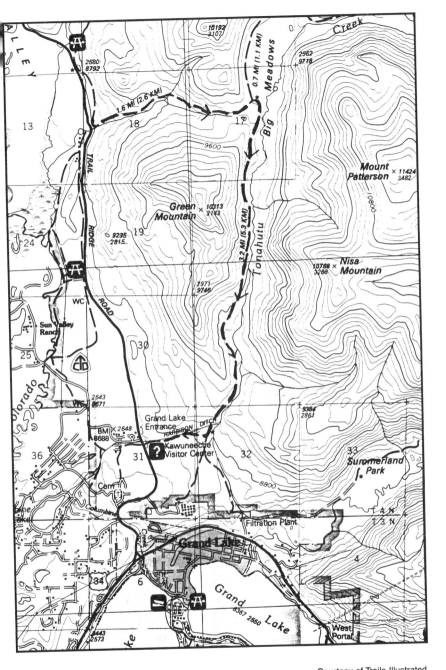

Courtesy of Trails Illustrated

81

20B Cub Lake and The Pool

Hike Distance: 5.8 miles (loop)
Hiking Time: 136 minutes total (Trailhead to Cub Lake in 56 minutes.
Cub Lake to The Pool in 32 minutes. The Pool to Cub
Lake Trailhead in 48 minutes.)
Starting Elevation: 8,080 feet
Highest Elevation: 8,755 feet (2,668 meters)
Elevation Gain: 895 feet (includes an extra 220 feet)
Difficulty: Easy
Steepness Index: 0.06
Trail: All the way
Relevant Maps: Longs Peak 7½ minute
McHenrys Peak 7½ minute
Trails Illustrated Number 200
Larimer County Number Three
Rocky Mountain National Park

Getting There: From Estes Park enter Rocky Mountain National Park by the Beaver Meadows Entrance. After 0.2 miles from the entrance station, go left onto the Bear Lake Road. At mile 1.5 from the entrance station turn right onto the Moraine Park Road. Follow this road for 1.6 miles to the Cub Lake Trailhead and park.

Cub Lake is a good early or late season hike. During the tourist season this area is very heavily used. The small elevation gain, the well defined trails, and the short distances make this a good choice for children and hikers who want less of a physical challenge. No pets or vehicles are permitted. A free map of this area may be obtained at the visitor center just outside the park entrance.

Start to the south past the trailhead sign and cross the river. The trail starts through a meadow before it ascends and curves to the southwest, passes the Cub Creek Campsite on the left and arrives at Cub Lake. The football field sized, lovely lake will be reached in about an hour. Continue up the trail on the north side of the lake to a high point overlooking the lake to reach a fork and a sign within ten more minutes. Take the right fork and descend one mile to The Pool, where the waters of the Big Thompson River flow into a small, deep pocket before continuing to the east. This makes a scenic and peaceful place for a rest stop before crossing the bridge and completing the loop in an easterly direction along the river back to the Fern Lake Trailhead. At one point you pass through some large boulders. The Fern Lake Trailhead is reached in about another half hour and the Cub Lake Trailhead in 15 minutes more to complete the loop.

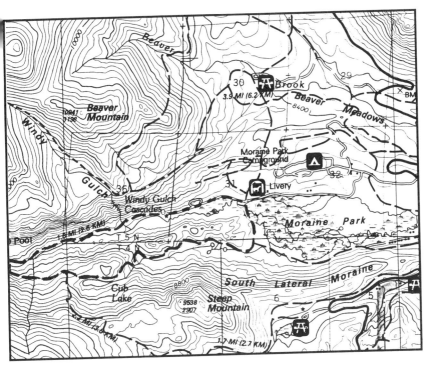

21A Twin Sisters Peaks

Hike Distance: 4.0 miles each way
Hiking Time: Up is 122 minutes. Down in 92 minutes.
Starting Elevation: 9,080 feet
Highest Elevation: 11,428 feet (3,483 meters)
Elevation Gain: 2390 feet (includes 42 extra feet)
Difficulty: Moderate
Steepness Index: 0.11
Trail: All the way
Relevant Maps: Longs Peak 7½ minute
                     Trails Illustrated Number 200
                     Larimer County Number Four
                     Roosevelt National Forest
                     Rocky Mountain National Park
Views from the Summit: N to Estes Park and Lake Estes
                     NW to YMCA Camp of the Rockies and Mount Ypsilon
                     E to Meadow, Willow, Mirror and Rainbow Lakes
                     SSW to Meadow Mountain
                     SW to Copeland Mountain, Mount Meeker, Longs Peak and Mount Lady Washington

Getting There: Either drive north from the town of Lyons where Colorado 7 and U.S. 36 intersect for 26.4 miles on Colorado 7 or south from Estes Park where Colorado 7 and U.S. 36 intersect for 8.2 miles on Colorado 7.

A sign on the east side of the road directs you to a parking area at the Twin Sisters Trailhead in 200 yards.

The hike to Twin Sisters to quite popular. Much of the route lies in a detached southeastern segment of Rocky Mountain National Park. The trail is clear and provides a gradual ascent to two adjacent summits and excellent vistas. Along the way there are occasional glimpses of Longs Peak and above timberline there are good views of Estes Park to the north.

No entrance fee is required but pets, vehicles and guns are forbidden on National Park land.

For the hike to the top, begin from the trailhead sign north of the parking area and proceed north northwest. This first trail segment crosses private property.

Follow the excellent main trail as it enters Rocky Mountain National Park property after one mile. Some interesting rock formations are passed as switchbacks take you to timberline where the western summit of Twin Sisters Peaks can be seen adjacent to a metal tower. You are now on National Forest land. Some cairns mark the trail as you ascend south to a saddle between the higher east summit on your left and the western high point on your right. A stone hut and radio tower lie on your right.

To reach the highest point turn left (east) at the saddle and lose a little elevation as you curve around the right side of a subpeak. A faint trail leads you over rocks to a U.S.G.S. marker on a rocky ridge at the top. The western summit is more easily reached from the saddle by a clearer trail. The views of the east face of Longs Peak can be excellent from either summit. Return by your ascent trail.

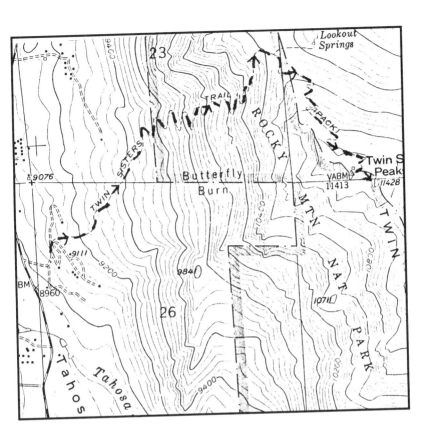

21B Bierstadt Lake

Hike Distance:	1.2 miles each way and 0.6 miles around lake.
Hiking Time:	Up is 30 minutes. Around lake in 14 minutes. Down in 25 minutes.
Starting Elevation:	8,870 feet
Highest Elevation:	9,430 feet (2,874 meters)
Elevation Gain:	620 feet (includes an extra 30 feet each way)
Difficulty:	Easy
Steepness Index:	0.09
Trail:	All the way
Relevant Maps:	Longs Peak 7½ minute
	Trails Illustrated Number 200
	Larimer County Number Three
	Rocky Mountain National Park

Getting There: Drive on U.S. 36 into Rocky Mountain National Park by way of the Beaver Meadows entrance. After 0.2 miles from the park entrance turn left onto the Bear Creek Road and drive toward Bear Lake Road for 6.4 miles to the parking area and the trailhead for Bierstadt Lake on the right.

Named after the German artist who painted many beautiful scenes of the American west, Bierstadt Lake is an easy destination within beautiful Rocky

Mountain National Park. Several switchbacks make for a gentle grade to this quiet lake with impressive peaks to the south. It makes a good hike for families.

Start your hike north northwest past the trailhead sign at the edge of the parking area. Ascend through some aspen and as you follow the switchbacks, take in the scenic valley to the south and southeast. The trail eventually descends to a fork and a trail sign. The left fork continues to Bear Lake. Take the right fork and in a few minutes arrive at Bierstadt Lake. A trail circles the lake. Take some time for reflection, refreshment and relating to the birds, ground squirrels and the scenery before your return.

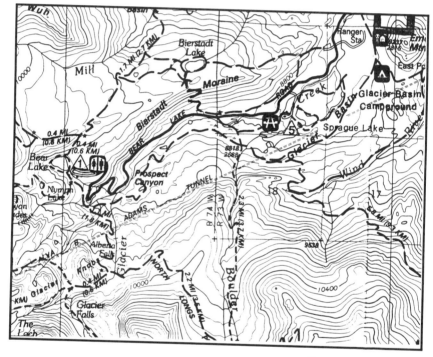

Courtesy of Trails Illustrated

22A Lower Boulder Lake

Hike Distance: 2.4 miles each way
Hiking Time: Up in 66 minutes. Down in 68 minutes.
Starting Elevation: 9,510 feet
Highest Elevation: 10,100 feet (3,078 meters)
Elevation Gain: 1,200 feet (includes 610 extra feet)
Difficulty: Easy
Steepness Index: 0.09
Trail: All the way
Relevant Maps: Willow Lakes 7½ minute
                      Summit County Number One
                      Arapaho National Forest
                      Trails Illustrated Number 108

Getting There: Drive from Exit 205 of Interstate 70 at Silverthorne and travel north on Colorado 9 for 7.9 miles. The Blue River Campground will be on the right. Turn left onto unpaved Summit County Road 1350 and ascend 1.4 miles to a fork. Go left onto the Rock Creek Road. Stay on the main road and keep right at 0.4 miles, 1.1 miles and 1.4 miles. The last fork leads you into a parking area and the Rock Creek Trailhead sign. Park here.

The Gore Range Trail extends for over 50 miles along the eastern slopes of the Gore Range from above Green Mountain Reservoir on the north to Copper Mountain on the south. This hike to secluded Lower Boulder Lake uses part of the Gore Range Trail and takes you up and down along a forest trail with few vistas until you reach the lake.

Your hike begins south from the trailhead sign and just past a trail register on the Rock Creek Trail. After 0.3 miles, take a right fork at a sign onto the Gore Range Trail. Follow this clear forest trail as it meanders up and down to the northwest. Pass through a lovely aspen grove and past some small ponds. After 0.5 miles on the Gore Range Trail keep right at a fork and a half mile later take a left fork and continue north northwest. In another half mile reach a T at a sign and ascend to the left. In a few hundred yards you will reach another fork. Both forks lead to the lake, so take your pick. After a little more ascent, you will see the lake with its sandy shore below. Around the lake are many good campsites. The trail continues beyond Lower Boulder Lake to the west southwest for almost 3 more miles to Upper Boulder Lake. Be sure to take the correct forks on your return hike.

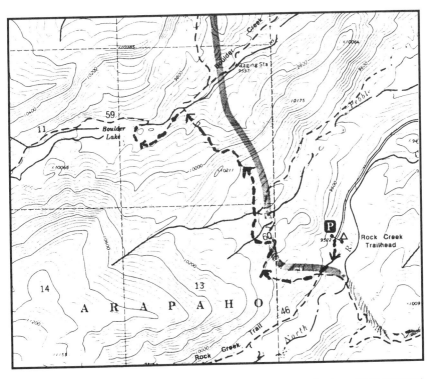

Courtesy of Trails Illustrated

22B Lost Lake

Hike Distance: 3.4 miles each way.
Hiking Time: Up in 88 minutes. Down in 80 minutes.
Starting Elevation: 9,627 feet
Highest Elevation: 10,244 feet (3,122 meters)
Elevation Gain: 807 feet (includes an extra 190 feet)
Difficulty: Easy
Steepness Index: 0.05
Trail: All the way
Relevant Maps: Trails Illustrated Number 108
     Vail West 7½ minute
     Eagle County Number Two
     White River National Forest

Getting There: Drive to Vail and leave Interstate 70 at Exit 176. Then proceed west for 1 mile on the frontage road north of the highway. Turn right onto the Red Sandstone Road and after 0.7 miles take the left fork which continues as the Red Sandstone Road. All distances given will be from the frontage road. Keep right at mile 3.2, left at mile 3.4 and right at mile 7.2 before parking in 100 more yards at the trailhead on the right. Regular cars can easily drive to this point.

Here is a good, easy lake hike for the early season in the lush Eagles Nest Wilderness. The destination is one of many, so-called Lost Lakes in Colorado. (A shorter trail also reaches this peaceful lake from the east via a spur off the Red Sandstone Road at mile 3.4 from the frontage road.) This route lies along a ridge, traverses some aspen groves, three open forested areas and requires only modest elevation gain.

Begin the hike to the northeast on the clear trail and continue through lovely forest on the ridge for two miles to a junction. The left fork leads down to Piney Lake. You continue straight and pass through several clear-cut areas before your gentle descent to peaceful Lost Lake. Keep right at a signed fork about four hundred yards before the lake.

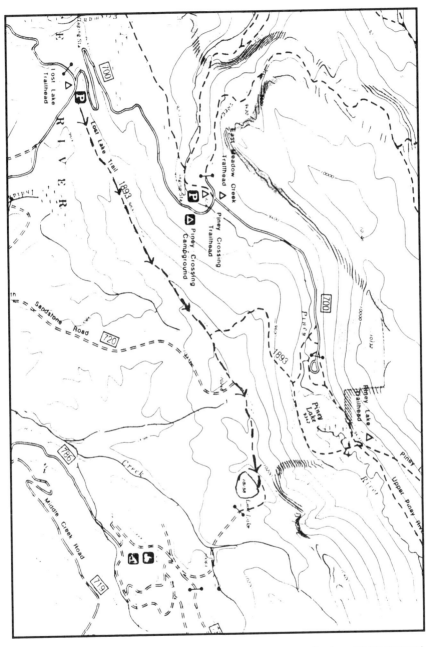

Courtesy of Trails Illustrated

89

23A Hartenstein Lake

Hike Distance:	3.0 miles each way.
Hiking Time:	Up in 96 minutes. Down in 72 minutes.
Starting Elevation:	9,900 feet
Highest Elevation:	11,451 feet (3,490 meters)
Elevation Gain:	1,711 feet (includes 80 feet of extra elevation gain each way)
Difficulty:	Moderate
Steepness Index:	0.11
Trail:	All the way
Relevant Maps:	Mount Yale 7½ minute
	Chaffee County Number Two
	San Isabel National Forest
	Trails Illustrated Number 129

Getting There: From Main Street in Buena Vista at the stoplight, drive west on Chaffee County 306 for 12.3 miles to the paved Denny Creek Trailhead parking area on your right. Park here. Denny Creek lies just to the east. (This road continues west over Cottonwood Pass to Taylor Park.)

Buena Vista is my idea of an ideal Colorado mountain town. Surrounded by towering peaks, adjacent to the San Isabel National Forest and close to good roads over many passes including Cottonwood, Monarch and Independence, it is an outdoor person's dream.

The hike to Hartenstein Lake begins off the improved Cottonwood Pass road that can be negotiated by regular cars all the way from Buena Vista to Taylor Park to the west. The lake is named after George K. Hartenstein, a Buena Vista lawyer at the turn of the century.

From Denny Creek trailhead at a sign and adjacent to toilet facilities, take the excellent trail up to the northwest. In one mile Denny Creek is crossed. A second crossing occurs soon thereafter and the trail then turns west. After two miles from the trailhead, you reach a sign pointing left to Hartenstein Lake (one mile), and straight ahead to Browns Pass (1.5 miles) and to Kroenke Lake (3.5 miles). Turn left (south southwest), cross a creek and follow the trail as it winds clockwise around a small hill to reach Hartenstein Lake from its north side in half an hour.

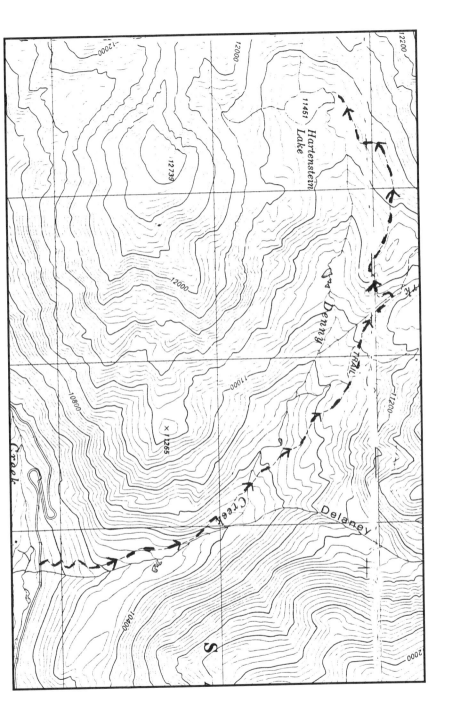

23B Ouzel Falls

Hike Distance:	2.7 miles each way.
Hiking Time:	Up in 70 minutes. Down in 65 minutes.
Starting Elevation:	8,500 feet
Highest Elevation:	9,400 feet (2,865 meters)
Elevation Gain:	1,060 feet (includes an extra 80 feet of elevation gain each way due to undulations in the trail)
Difficulty:	Easy
Steepness Index:	0.07
Trail:	All the way
Relevant Maps:	Allens Park 7½ minute
	Boulder County
	Rocky Mountain National Park
	Roosevelt National Forest
	Trails Illustrated Number 200

Getting There: From the junction of U.S. 36 and Colorado 7 at the west end of Lyons, Colorado, drive west and north on Colorado 7 for 21.2 miles and turn left at the sign to the Wild Basin Ranger Station. Continue for 0.4 miles on the paved road and turn right on the dirt road at another Wild Basin Ranger Station sign. Continue on this excellent dirt road for 2.2 miles to the end of the road at a parking area and the trailhead at the Wild Basin Ranger Station.

There may be better hikes along flowing water than this hike to Ouzel Falls but I don't know of one. With the heavy spring run-off, this hike shows you a riot of rampaging water. It's an ideal outing for families since it's neither too long nor too steep and no National Park fee is required.

Begin at the trailhead sign and proceed south southwest over a bridge across Hunters Creek. Continue on the excellent trail and within ten minutes pass Copeland Falls on the left. Keep right and ascend with the raging creek on your left until you cross a large wooden bridge and then ascend more steeply to reach the Calypso Cascades, where water rages steeply downward over the boulders and passes beneath a series of three wooden bridges. Continue west over these bridges and soon pass a burn area on your left and eventually walk through this burn area which resulted from a 1978 fire. Longs Peak and Mount Meeker may be visible to the north northwest. In about one mile from the Calypso Cascades you will reach Ouzel Falls and another wooden bridge. A three minute hike along the left side of Ouzel Creek leads to the base of the falls and a great place for a break. (The trail continues farther to a fork with the left trail leading to Ouzel and Bluebird Lakes and the right going to Thunder Lake if you have the time, interest and energy.)

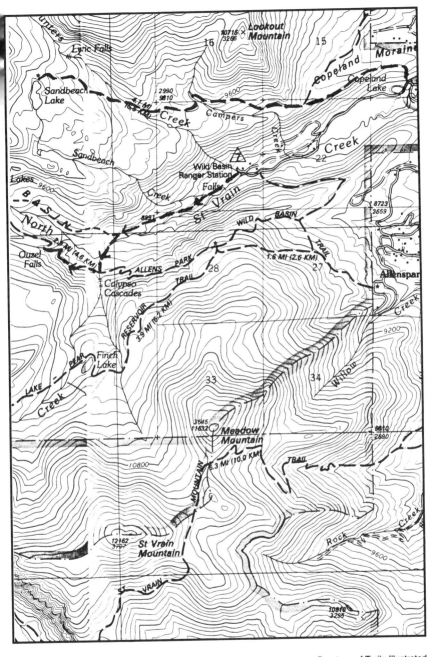

Courtesy of Trails Illustrated

24A Deer Mountain (Rocky Mountain National Park)

Hike Distance: 3.0 miles each way.
Hiking Time: Up in 83 minutes. Down in 72 minutes.
Starting Elevation: 8,930 feet
Highest Elevation: 10,013 feet (3,052 meters)
Elevation Gain: 1,333 feet (includes 250 feet of extra elevation gain)
Difficulty: Moderate
Steepness Index: 0.10
Trail: All the way
Relevant Maps: Estes Park 7½ minute
                      Larimer County Number Three
                      Roosevelt National Forest
                      Rocky Mountain National Park
                      Trails Illustrated Number 200
Views from the Summit: NW to Mount Ypsilon, Mount Fairchild, Hagues Peak
                       and Mummy Mountain
                       ENE to Estes Park and Lake Estes
                       ESE to Marys Lake
                       S to Longs Peak
                       SSE to YMCA Camp of the Rockies and Estes Cone
                       SE to Twin Sisters Peaks and Lily Mountain
                       SW to Hallett Peak and Flattop Mountain

Getting There: From the Beaver Meadows Entrance to Rocky Mountain
National Park, drive west. Keep right at a fork in 0.2 miles and continue for
2.9 miles farther to the trailhead and a parking area on your right. An intersection and the eastern entrance to Trail Ridge Road lies about 100 yards
to the west.

Rocky Mountain National Park is a wonderful, natural resource just two hours
from Denver by car. Filled with pretty lakes, impressive mountains and clearly
marked trails, the park is popular with tourists but should not be overlooked
by Coloradans. An entrance fee is required.

The Deer Mountain trail is one of the easier summit routes in the park and
is recommended for families.

Begin north from the trailhead. The trail quickly curves to the east and rises
through timber in a series of switchbacks to a saddle and then descends to
the east to reach a large pile of rocks and a sign at a fork in the trail. This
point lies 2.8 miles from the trailhead. Turn right and ascend southwest to
reach a great overlook at the high point. A huge cairn and a nearby U.S.G.S.
marker indicate the summit.

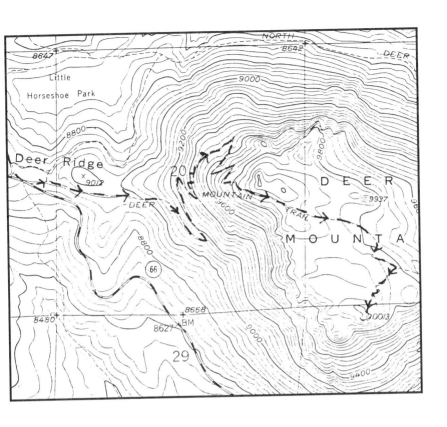

24B Gibson Lake

Hike Distance:	2.5 miles each way
Hiking Time:	Up in 80 minutes. Down in 60 minutes.
Starting Elevation:	10,316 feet
Highest Elevation:	11,860 feet (3,615 meters)
Elevation Gain:	1,614 feet (includes 35 feet of extra elevation gain each way)
Difficulty:	Moderate
Steepness Index:	0.12
Trail:	All the way
Relevant Maps:	Jefferson 7½ minute
	Park County Number One
	Pike National Forest

Getting There: From U.S. 285 at the ghost town of Webster (3.2 miles west of Grant or 4.4 miles east of Kenosha Pass), turn west on Road 120 and drive up Hall Valley for 5.3 miles past the Handcart Campground to the Hall Valley Campground. En route take the right fork at 3.3 miles and the left fork at 5.2 miles. Continue past the Hall Valley Campground on the rough road up the gulch for 1.25 miles farther and park in the designated area on the left. Regular cars can come this far.

Gibson Lake lies at the foot of Whale Peak which is accessible by trail south from the lake and then west and northwest parallel to the ridge. Gibson Lake drains into the North Fork of the South Platte River.

Follow the trail which begins west of the parking area at a sign. Descend to the south, cross the creek on a small, wooden bridge and continue southwest and then west up the valley on the clear trail which keeps to the right of the creek until you cross it near timberline. In about 1.3 miles from the trailhead, take a left fork and stay lower in the valley and closer to the creek. In 1.2 more miles you will arrive at Gibson Lake situated in a bowl beneath Whale Peak to your west southwest. If you lose the trail, just continue to ascend close to the creek which will lead you to the lake.

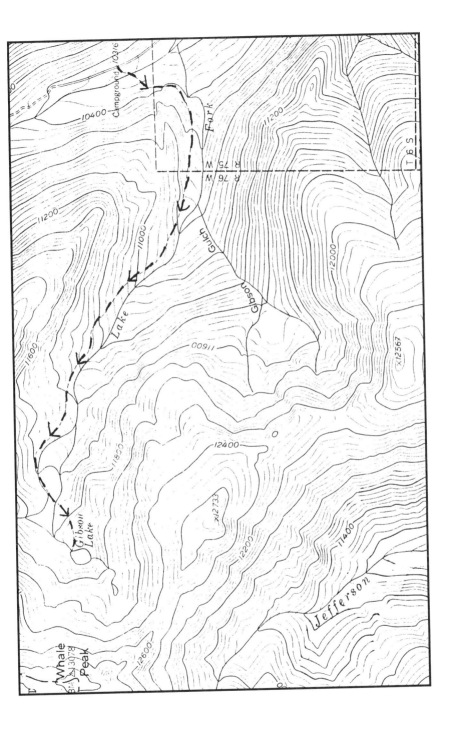

25A Herman Lake

Hike Distance:	3.0 miles each way.
Hiking Time:	Up in 105 minutes. Down in 80 minutes.
Starting Elevation:	10,280 feet
Highest Elevation:	12,000 feet (3,658 meters)
Elevation Gain:	1,920 feet (includes an extra 100 feet of elevation gain each way)
Difficulty:	Moderate
Steepness Index:	0.12
Trail:	All the way
Relevant Maps:	Grays Peak 7½ minute
	Loveland Pass 7½ minute
	Clear Creek County
	Arapaho National Forest
	Trails Illustrated Number 104

Getting There: Drive on Interstate 70 between the Eisenhower-Johnson Tunnel on the west and Bakerville on the east to Exit 218. Park in the large flat area northeast of the highway. The trailhead lies about 400 yards to the east of the entrance to this area.

By late June the higher valleys of Colorado become resplendent with many varieties of exquisite, colorful flowers. The Herman Gulch trailhead is less than an hour from Denver and is an excellent place to view these flowers, camp or have a family backpack picnic. The initial part of this hike is a bit steep as is the last section before reaching Herman Lake. Although you never need to use your hands for balance, there are several easy creek crossings and there are impressive peaks in every direction from the lake which is above timberline.

From the trailhead at the parking area begin on the excellent trail and ascend to the northeast. A map and trail register are quickly encountered on the left. Within five minutes from the parking area take the left fork and ascend to the west. (The right fork is another good hike up Watrous Gulch.) The trail continues northwest up the gulch with the main creek always on your left. Eventually just before timberline the route turns steeply to the north to gain a flat area with two ponds near the trail as you head west to the lake at the foot of Pettingell Peak. The lake lies lower than the high point of the trail. Pettingell Peak lies west northwest. Citadel Peak (the unoffical name of a 13,294 foot peak) is southwest. Mount Bethel lies southeast and Mount Parnassus is northeast.

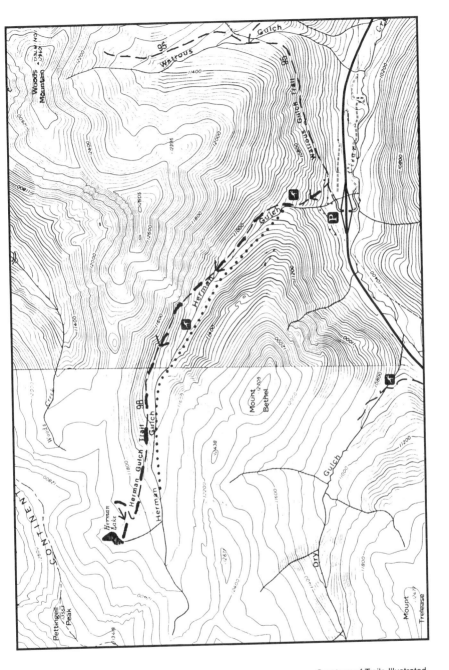

Courtesy of Trails Illustrated

99

25B Lulu City

Hike Distance:	3.1 miles each way.
Hiking Time:	Up in 82 minutes. Down in 80 minutes.
Starting Elevation:	9,060 feet
Highest Elevation:	9,340 feet (2,847 meters)
Elevation Gain:	660 feet (includes an extra 190 feet of elevation gain each way due to undulations in the trail)
Difficulty:	Easy
Steepness Index:	0.04
Trail:	All the way
Relevant Maps:	Fall River Pass 7½ minute
	Grand County Number Two
	Rocky Mountain National Park
	Roosevelt National Forest
	Trails Illustrated Number 200

Getting There: The Colorado River Trailhead is reached by driving on Trail Ridge Road (U.S. 34) in Rocky Mountain National Park either 10.9 miles south from the Alpine Visitor Center or about 12 miles north from Grand Lake. The paved side road leads northwest 0.1 mile to a parking area at the trailhead.

Lulu City flourished between 1879 and 1883 until hopes for mining success were dashed. The population never exceeded 200. Now there are few remnants left of the settlement. The ruins of some cabins can be found in the flat grassy meadow on the east side of the nascent Colorado River.

Begin hiking north northwest from the northwestern end of the parking area. The trail is clear and well-marked as it passes along the eastern banks of the Colorado River. Take the right fork after a half mile from the trailhead and 1.3 miles later pass the Shipler Cabin ruins on your right. In 1.1 more miles take a left fork and descend 0.2 miles to the meadow site where Lulu City once stood. Explore the area and maybe have a picnic. This is a good hike for families. The Never Summer Mountain Range lies west of your route to Lulu City and some of its imposing summits may be visible during your hike. (The trail will fork above Lulu City and continue either north to Poudre Pass or northwest to Thunder Pass.)

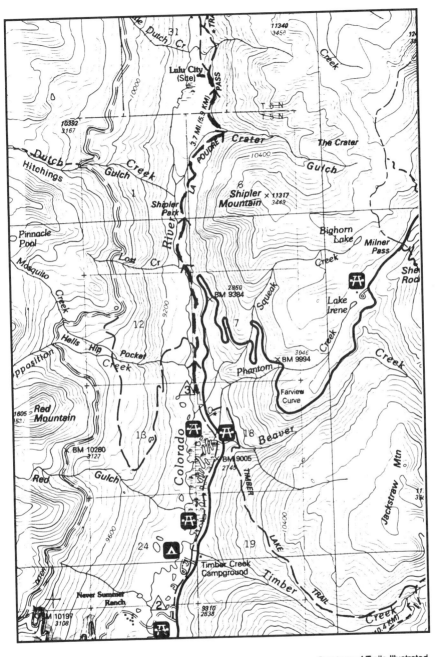

Courtesy of Trails Illustrated

26A St. Vrain Mountain

Hike Distance:	5.0 miles each way.
Hiking Time:	Up in 165 minutes. Down in 100 minutes.
Starting Elevation:	8,800 feet
Highest Elevation:	12,162 feet (3,707 meters)
Elevation Gain:	3,432 feet (includes an extra 35 feet each way)
Difficulty:	Moderate
Steepness Index:	0.13
Trail:	Initial 4.4 miles
Relevant Maps:	Allens Park 7½ minute
	Boulder County
	Roosevelt National Forest
	Trails Illustrated Number 200
Views from the Summit:	NNE to Twin Sisters Peaks and Meadow Mountain
	NNW to Longs Peak, Mount Meeker, Sandbeach Lake, and Finch Lake
	NW to McHenrys Peak, Chiefs Head Peak, and Pagoda Mountain
	S to Mount Audubon
	SSW to Mount Toll and Paiute Peak
	SE to Green Mountain, Bear Peak, South Boulder Peak, and Beaver Reservoir
	W to Copeland Mountain

Getting There: From the intersection of U.S. 36 and Colorado 7 at the west end of Lyons, drive on Colorado 7 for 18.6 miles to Allenspark and turn left. Follow the paved road as it curves to the left for 0.2 miles and then turn right onto Ski Road Co. Road 107 which is unpaved. Follow this main road as it passes many private homes and runs parallel to Rock Creek on the left. After 1.8 miles from Colorado 7 take the right fork at a sign and in 0.5 miles farther park in the designated area just past the St. Vrain Mountain trailhead. Regular cars can reach this parking area.

St. Vrain Mountain is named after Ceran St. Vrain, a trader in the early days of Colorado. The summit forms part of the current southern boundary of Rocky Mountain National Park.

Start your hike to the southwest from the trailhead sign. The good trail ascends gradually and you will pass an Indian Peaks Wilderness sign after a half mile. Rock Creek will soon be nearby on your left and an easy creek crossing will occur higher in the basin. One mile after this crossing you will see St. Vrain Mountain resembling an ant hill to the southwest. In 0.6 miles farther you will pass a large cairn on the left and soon thereafter a sign which states that you are entering Rocky Mountain National Park. Follow the trail for 0.6 miles farther and then leave the trail and proceed southwest (right) up the ridge to the top. Try to avoid the scrub oak below timberline. There are two rock shelters at the summit. If the weather is right, there are magnificent views into the Indian Peaks and Rocky Mountain National Park. Retrace your route to descend.

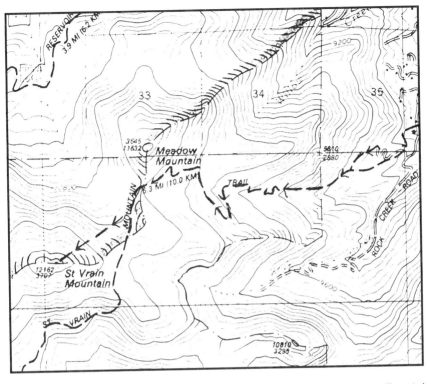

Courtesy of Trails Illustrated

26B Lenawee Mountain

Hike Distance:	4.4 miles each way.
Hiking Time:	Up in 120 minutes. Down in 70 minutes.
Starting Elevation:	10,350 feet
Highest Elevation:	13,204 feet (4,025 meters)
Elevation Gain:	2,874 feet (includes 10 feet extra each way)
Difficulty:	Moderate
Steepness Index:	0.12
Trail:	Initial 3.4 miles
Relevant Maps:	Montezuma 7½ minute
	Grays Peak 7½ minute
	Summit County Number Two
	Arapaho National Forest
	Trails Illustrated Number 104
Views from the Summit:	N to Mount Sniktau
	NNE to Grizzly Peak
	NNW to Loveland Pass
	NE to Torreys Peak and Grays Peak
	NW to Arapaho Basin Ski Area

Getting There: Drive on U.S. 6 either 7.7 miles east from Exit 205 of Interstate 70 or 8.5 miles southwest from Loveland Pass and turn south on the access road to the Keystone Ski Area. Within 100 yards turn left onto

103

the paved Montezuma Road and drive for 4.6 miles from U.S. 6. Then turn left onto a good dirt road and drive for 1.7 miles up Peru Gulch. En route keep left at a fork at mile 1.0, cross Peru Creek and park off the road near the trailhead signs. Regular cars can come this far.

This is a moderately steep hike to a ridge and a peak overlooking three lovely mountain valleys. The off-trail portion of this hike is above timberline and proceeds easily to a grassy ridge and the Lenawee Mountain summit which can be seen to the north throughout the second half of the hike.

Start the hike to the northwest from a trail register. After 0.5 miles take a right fork and pass a cabin ruin on your left. After 1.0 mile farther, take another right fork at an overlook as the trail briefly turns to the east. Soon pass timberline and several cairns which help mark the sometimes faint trail. Lenawee Mountain will now be visible to the north. After 3.4 miles leave the trail just before it begins a steady descent and ascend to the north northeast (right) to gain the ridge and then go left over talus to the unmarked high point of the ridge. The trail which you left continues up Thurman Gulch to cross an unnamed pass and continue down to the Arapaho Basin Ski Area. Retrace your ascent route for the return to your car at the trailhead.

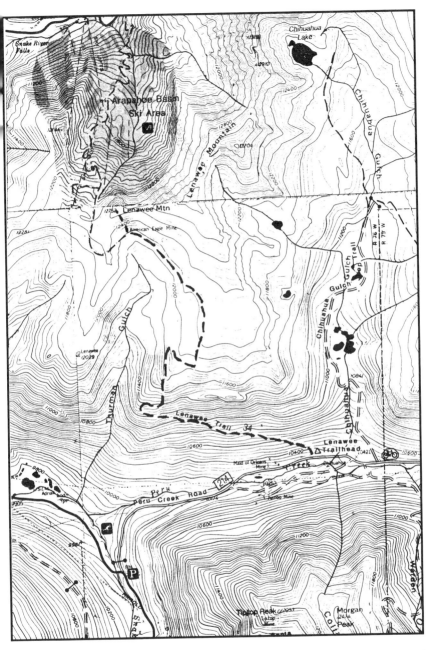

Courtesy of Trails Illustrated

SELECTED PHOTOGRAPHS

Upper Pennsylvania Creek 1A

Mount Sniktau from
Herman Gulch 25A

Saint Vrain Mountain 26A

West from Mount Sherman 27A

James Peak from the East 27B

Quandary Peak 29A

Mummy Mountain from Lawn Lake Trail 31B

Approaching Bowen Pass 33A

Alberta Falls 35A

Crestone Needle and Crestone Peak from Kit Carson Peak 35B

Humboldt Peak from Kit Carson Peak 35B

Approaching Mount Irving Hale 36A

Mount Toll and Blue Lake 38A

Finch Lake and Copeland Mountain 38B

Timber Lake 40B

Holy Cross City 44A

27A Mount Sherman

Hike Distance:	2.5 miles each way
Hiking Time:	Up in 100 minutes. Down in 70 minutes.
Starting Elevation:	11,960 feet
Highest Elevation:	14,036 feet (4,278 meters)
Elevation Gain:	2,206 feet (includes an extra 65 feet of elevation gain each way)
Difficulty:	Moderate
Steepness Index:	0.17
Trail:	All the way
Relevant Maps:	Mount Sherman 7½ minute
	Park County Number One
	Pike National Forest
	Trails Illustrated Number 110
Views from the Summmit:	N to Gemini Peak
	NNE to Mount Lincoln, Mount Bross and Mount Democrat
	NNW to Pacific Peak
	NE to Mount Silverheels
	NW to Mount of the Holy Cross
	E to Pikes Peak
	ESE to White Ridge
	SSE to the Buffalo Peaks and Horseshoe Mountain
	SW to West Sheridan, Mount Elbert and Mount Massive
	SSW to Mount Sheridan, Mount Harvard and Twin Lakes
	W to Leadville and Turquoise Lake
	WNW to East Ball Mountain, West Dyer Mountain and Dyer Mountain

Getting There: From the intersection of U.S. 285 and Colorado 9 at the east edge of Fairplay, drive south on U.S. 285 for 1.3 miles and turn right onto the Fourmile Creek Road which is Park County Road 18. Keep left at mile 1.2 and eventually pass Horseshoe Campground on your left and Fourmile Campground on your right. Keep right at mile 10.7 and straight at mile 11.2. Park off the road around mile 12.0 since the road gets rougher and is blocked in 0.4 more miles. Regular cars can come as far as mile 12.0 from U.S. 285 on this good dirt road.

Mount Sherman is named after the Civil War general, William Tecumseh Sherman. It forms part of the boundary between Lake and Park Counties. There are 54 Colorado mountains which are fourteen thousand feet or higher. Many hikers have hiked to the top of all of them. Some, including the Smith Family, have ascended all of them in 54 consecutive days. This is one of the easier fourteeners since the entire hike is above timberline and the distance to the top is modest.

Begin your hike by ascending the rough dirt road to the northwest. You will soon pass around a metal road barrier to reach the site of the former Dauntless Mine. Continue up on the road to the highest abandoned mine in the area, the Hilltop Mine. From there follow the road which curves to the north-west and continues as a faint trail. Either follow this trail up over lots of loose rock, known as scree, or ascend more to the west to gain the ridge at a lower elevation. When you have reached the ridge, turn north northeast on the trail which lies on the east side of the ridge. Pass a false summit and finally reach the top which is marked by a small cairn, a rock shelter and a register cylinder. Sign in and take in the exceptional view before returning by your ascent route.

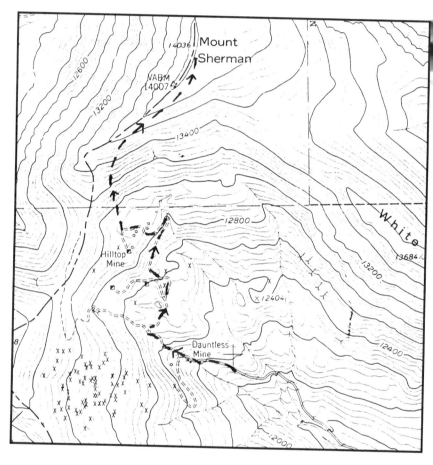

27B James Peak

Hike Distance:	3.0 miles each way.
Hiking Time:	Up in 142 minutes. Down in 96 minutes.
Starting Elevation:	10,385 feet
Highest Elevation:	13,294 feet (4,052 meters)
Elevation Gain:	2,969 feet (includes an extra 30 feet each way)
Difficulty:	Moderate
Steepness Index:	0.15
Trail:	Initial 0.8 mile and intermittent after St. Marys Glacier
Relevant Maps:	Empire 7½ minute
	Clear Creek County
	Arapaho National Forest
	Trails Illustrated Number 103
Views from the Summit:	NNW to Longs Peak and Heart Lake
	NW to Winter Park and Fraser and Parkview Mountain
	SSE to Square Top Mountain
	SSW to Grays Peak, Torreys Peak, Mount Bancroft and Mount Eva
	SE to Mount Evans and Mount Bierstadt
	SW to Parry Peak
	W to Winter Park Ski Area and Bottle Peak
	WSW to Bills Peak and Byers Peak

Getting There: Via Exit 238 from Interstate 70 just west of Idaho Springs, drive northwest up Fall River Road for 9.0 miles and park in either of two parking areas on each side of the road. The road is paved to these parking areas and even somewhat farther.

This hike to James Peak is unusual because it involves crossing 0.3 miles of the St. Marys Glacier. This is a very popular area. Skiers and snowboarders often come here to work on their off-season technique.

James Peak lies on the Continental Divide and forms part of the boundary between three counties, Clear Creek, Grand and Gilpin. The mountain is named after the early Colorado botanist, Edwin James.

Begin hiking up the paved road and take a very quick left turn up a rough rocky road. You will encounter several forks but stay on this main road and always ascend. The road arrives at St. Marys Lake after 0.6 miles and continues past its eastern border to reach St. Marys Glacier. Hike as far north as you can before turning left (west northwest) and traversing the snowfield which is about 0.3 miles long. Be sure to get good footholds for the gradual ascent. Continue to the end of the snow and reach a large valley with James Peak looming impressively to the west. There will be little if any trail at this point as you continue west over the tundra and pass to the right of a large, rocky outcropping. After crossing some four-wheel drive roads, reach a road at the base of James Peak. Follow this road as it gradually winds in a clockwise direction up James Peak. The road ends before the summit. Continue to ascend to the north to reach the flat summit area. The high point is marked by a metal pole in a cairn and a register cylinder. An intermittent trail which stays closer to the ridge and parallels the rocky road also rises to the summit.

The descent retraces your ascent route. Be sure to keep left of the rocky outcropping en route back to the glacier and the trailhead.

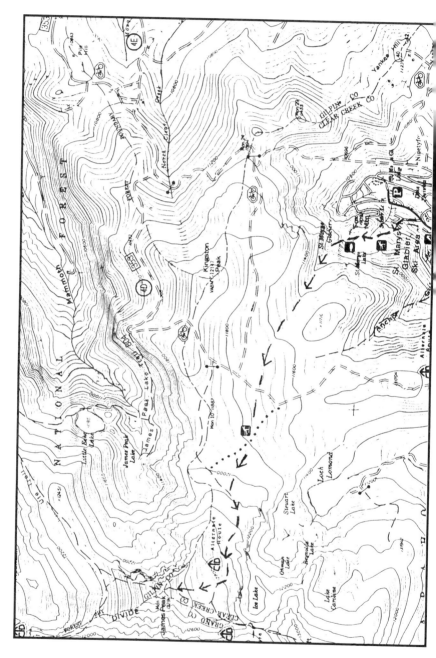

Courtesy of Trails Illustrated

28A Square Top Mountain

Hike Distance: 4.7 miles each way.
Hiking Time: Up in 155 minutes. Down in 98 minutes.
Starting Elevation: 11,669 feet (Guanella Pass)
Highest Elevation: 13,794 feet (4,204 meters)
Elevation Gain: 2,565 feet (includes 220 extra feet each way)
Difficulty: Moderate
Steepness Index: 0.10
Trail: First 3.3 miles
Relevant Maps: Mount Evans 7½ minute
                     Montezuma 7½ minute
                     Clear Creek County
                     Pike National Forest
                     Trails Illustrated Number 104
Views from the Summit: N to Longs Peak, Mount Wilcox, and Silver Dollar
                     Lake
                     NE to Sugarloaf Peak
                     NW to Grays Peak, Torreys Peak, and Argentine
                     Peak
                     E to Mount Bierstadt
                     ENE to Gray Wolf Mountain, Mount Rogers, Mount
                     Spalding and Mount Evans
                     S to South Park
                     SE to Geneva Mountain, Mount Logan, North Twin
                     Cone Peak and Pikes Peak
                     SW to Mount of the Holy Cross
                     WSW to Uneva Peak, Buffalo Mountain and Red
                     Peak.

Getting There: Drive to Guanella Pass either 10.7 miles south from the four-way stop signs in the middle of Georgetown or 13.4 miles north from U.S. 285 at Grant via Park County Road 62 and park on the east side of the pass. Regular cars can reach Guanella Pass.

By July the snow has melted and tall mountains like Square Top can be reached. You can get a high start on this hike from Guanella Pass and the entire hike is above the trees. Lower Square Top Lake is passed midway. Being almost a "fourteener," Square Top Mountain offers special summit views.

Hike west from the parking area across the road and keep right at a fork which is reached in 100 yards. In another 100 yards take a left fork and another left fork 0.3 miles from the trailhead. You will generally be heading southwest toward the ridge running northwest to southeast up Square Top Mountain. The trail rises and falls before reaching the south edge of Lower Square Top Lake in 2.3 miles from the trailhead. Follow the trail up to the ridge where it ends. Then ascend southwest over the tundra and reach the summit ridge in 0.9 miles from the trail's end. It is a half mile west southwest on the ridge to the summit which is marked by a large cairn and a register cylinder. The best way down is to use the ascent route.

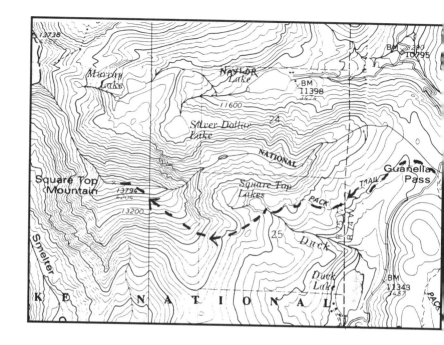

28B Devils Thumb Pass

Hike Distance:	4.1 miles each way
Hiking Time:	Out in 88 minutes. Back in 90 minutes.
Starting Elevation:	11,671 feet (Rollins Pass)
Highest Elevation:	12,000 feet (3,658 meters)
Elevation Gain:	1,113 feet (includes an extra 392 feet of elevation gain each way)
Difficulty:	Moderate
Steepness Index:	0.05
Trail:	All the way
Relevant Maps:	East Portal 7½ minute
	Grand County Number Four
	Arapaho National Forest
	Trails Illustrated Number 103

Getting There: Drive on U.S. 40 either 11.8 miles north from Berthoud Pass or 1.75 miles south from Vasquez Road in Winter Park. Turn northwest onto the road to Rollins Pass, which is designated Road 149. Stay on this good, main dirt road for 13.4 miles to a parking area and signs at Rollins Pass. En route keep right at mile 3.7, straight at mile 3.8, right at mile 4.5, straight at a 4-way intersection at mile 6.6 and right at mile 8.6, right at mile 8.8 and left at mile 13.3. Regular cars can drive all the way to Rollins Pass from U.S. 40.

Here is a scenic ridge walk above timberline between two passes on the Continental Divide Trail. Vehicles are forbidden on the trail and dogs must be kept on a leash. The hike begins at the town site of Corona which had a railroad station, hotel, restaurant and workers quarters until abandoned in

1928. The route parallels the Continental Divide which is the boundary between Grand and Boulder Counties and the Arapaho and Roosevelt National Forests.

From the parking area begin west northwest on the trail. Quickly pass an Indian Peaks Wilderness sign and a stone foundation. Descend to a fork and a side trail which goes down to King Lake on your right. Continue north up the ridge and follow the trail and frequent cairns over tundra and occasional talus along the west side of the ridge. There are at least two parallel trails which lead to another ridge and a final descent to a Continental Divide Trail sign on a pole just west of Devils Thumb Pass which is 11,747 feet high. Devils Thumb Lake will be seen to the east and the town of Tabernash to the west southwest. The rocky pinnacle, known as Devils Thumb, is located northeast of the pass and can be better appreciated by walking north up the ridge from the pass for a few hundred yards. To return, follow the cairns back to your vehicle at Rollins Pass.

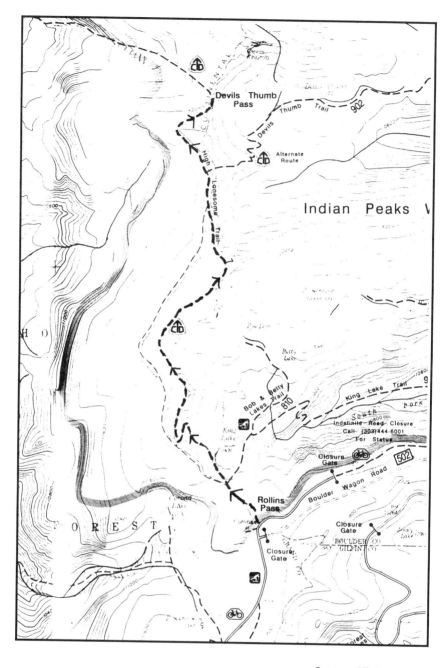

Courtesy of Trails Illustrated

29A Quandary Peak

Hike Distance:	2.9 miles each way.
Hiking Time:	Up in 138 minutes. Down in 112 minutes.
Starting Elevation:	10,900 feet
Highest Elevation:	14,265 feet (4,348 meters)
Elevation Gain:	3,365 feet
Difficulty:	Moderate
Steepness Index:	0.22
Trail:	All the way
Relevant Maps:	Breckenridge 7½ minute
	Summit County Number Two
	Arapaho National Forest
	Trails Illustrated Number 109

Views from the Summit: NNE to Mount Helen
NNW to Crystal Peak, Peak 10, Peak 9 and Peak 8
NE to Torreys Peak, Grays Peak and Bald Mountain
NW to Pacific Peak
SSE to the Monte Cristo Lakes, Mount Bross, Mount Lincoln and Cameron Peak
SE to Mount Silverheels and South Park
SW to Mount Democrat, North Star Mountain, La Plata Peak, Mount Elbert and Mount Massive
W to Fletcher Mountain, Mount Sopris and Mount of the Holy Cross
WSW to Snowmass Mountain and Capitol Peak

Getting There: From the Bell Tower in Breckenridge, drive south on Colorado 9 for 7.9 miles. Turn right onto a dirt road at a stop sign and a Road 850 sign. Avoiding a quick right fork, which leads to McCullough Gulch, continue west on the road for a total of .25 miles from Colorado 9 where two roads go off to your right. Park around here off the road.

Colorado is full of wonderful mountains to climb but the "fourteeners" get most of the attention. Here is the route up one of the easier of these elite peaks. Quandary Peak is the thirteenth highest in the state. The route is clear and there are no special dangers on the trail which leads all the way to the summit.

From the trailhead take the road on the north side of the main road (which leads to the Monte Cristo Lakes). Ascend northwest on this old mining road and in a few hundred yards take a right fork and ascend northeast. You will pass around a chain which blocks vehicular access. Go past two cabin ruins and follow the trail which rises steeply to the north with old mine diggings on your left. About 0.2 miles from the trailhead take a left fork at a pile of rocks and ascend steeply to the west. In 0.4 more miles you pass timberline on this ridge trail leading west northwest over tundra and talus (midsized rocks). If you lose the trail at any point on your ascent, just gain the ridge and continue west toward the summit which is visible most of the time. At the top are two open rock shelters and a U.S.G.S. marker in between. A register cylinder can be found in the more easterly shelter. The number of recognizable high peaks from this summit is rather large. Unless you are especially experienced and prepared, return by your ascent route and avoid the steep south ridges of Quandary.

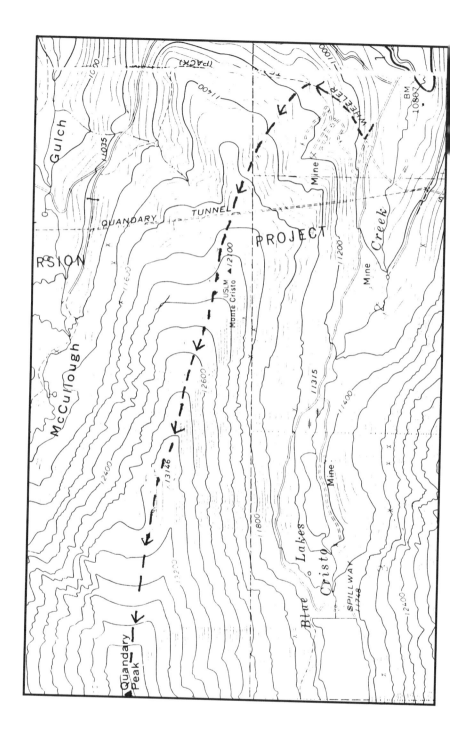

29B Booth Lake

Hike Distance:	5.3 miles each way
Hiking Time:	Up in 163 minutes. Down in 109 minutes.
Starting Elevation:	8,400 feet
Highest Elevation:	11,470 feet (3,496 meters)
Elevation Gain:	2,270 feet (includes an extra 100 feet each way)
Difficulty:	Moderate
Steepness Index:	0.12
Trail:	All the way
Relevant Maps:	Vail East 7½ minute
	Eagle County Number Two
	White River National Forest
	Trails Illustrated Number 108

Getting There: Take Exit 180 from Interstate 70 on the east side of Vail. Then take the access road on the north side of the highway and drive west for 0.8 miles and turn right on Booth Falls Road. Follow this road north for 0.2 miles to a parking area near the trailhead. Take the left fork just before you reach this parking area.

This hike will tax your endurance but the rewards are great. The incline is moderately steep over most of the route but there are several waterfalls including impressive Booth Falls at mile 2.1, many wildflowers and a spring at mile 3.2 en route to lovely Booth Lake in a steep bowl at the upper end of the valley.

Start your ascent northward from the parking area past the trailhead sign and register. You will pass through an aspen grove and cross a few small side creeks. Booth Creek will be on your left all the way up to the lake. Two miles from the trailhead, a left fork leads down a side trail to a sensational overlook of Booth Falls. Either retrace your route to the main trail or ascend more directly east to rejoin the trail and continue your trip north up the valley. In just under a mile from the falls you will cross a small creek as the trail passes along the eastern bank of Booth Creek. The trail then ascends a few hundred yards and the spring will be on your right. Just past the spring, the trail forks at a sign. Keep right. (The left fork crosses Booth Creek as the Piney River Trail.) Continue high up in the basin until the trail reaches the northern edge of Booth Lake close to timberline. The banks of the lake are a good place for a picnic, some photographs and reflection before you follow the trail back down to the trailhead.

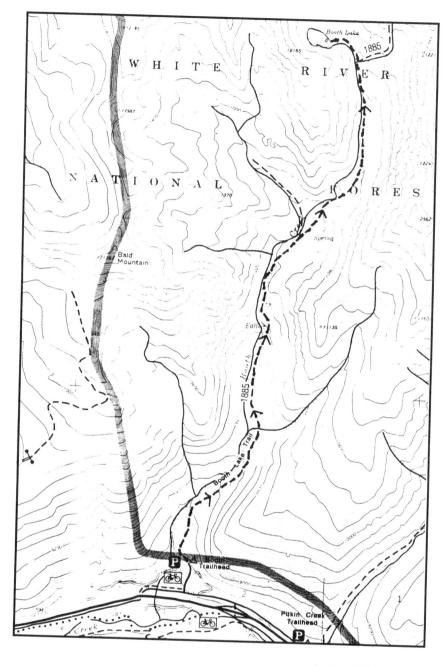

30A Pawnee Pass

Hike Distance:	4.2 miles each way
Hiking Time:	Up in 136 minutes. Down in 122 minutes.
Starting Elevation:	10,520 feet
Highest Elevation:	12,541 feet (3,822 meters)
Elevation Gain:	2,121 feet (includes an extra 50 feet of elevation gain each way)
Difficulty:	Moderate
Steepness Index:	0.10
Trail:	All the way
Relevant Maps:	Monarch Lake 7½ minute
	Ward 7½ minute
	Boulder County
	Roosevelt National Forest
	Trails Illustrated Number 102

Getting There: From the town of Nederland (west of Boulder) drive northwest on Colorado 72 for 12.0 miles and turn left onto the Brainard Lake Road. Continue on this good, paved road for 5.7 miles to the Long Lake Trailhead parking area. En route, turn right at mile 4.7 and left at mile 4.8 and drive around the right side of Brainard Lake. Then turn right at mile 5.3 and left at mile 5.4.

Pawnee Pass lies in the Indian Peaks Wilderness and forms part of the Continental Divide. The excellent trail is very popular and passes beside and above two beautiful lakes, Long Lake and Lake Isabelle. The mountains in this area are distinctive and there is abundant flowing water and lush vegetation.

Begin southwest at the trailhead signs and in a few hundred yards keep right as Long Lake appears on your left. In one mile from the trailhead take a right fork at a sign and continue west toward Pawnee Pass. In another mile lovely Lake Isabelle will be on your left. Take the right fork at a sign and ascend several switchbacks above Lake Isabelle and in two more miles reach the pass and a large sign. (The trail continues west and down to Pawnee Lake and eventually Monarch Lake.) The pass is a large, tundra covered, flat area with Pawnee Peak a half mile above to the north. Return to the Long Lake Trailhead as you came up.

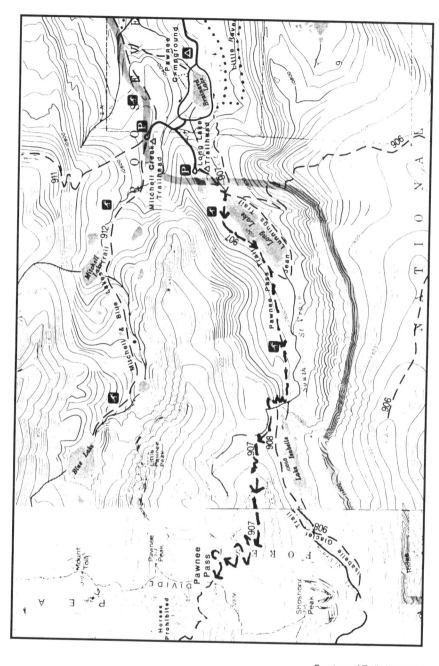

Courtesy of Trails Illustrated

128

30B Mount Shavano 14,229 Feet and Tabeguache Peak 14,155 Feet

Hike Distance:	Trailhead to Mount Shavano 5.2 miles. Mount Shavano to Tabeguache Peak 1.1 miles.
Hiking Time:	Trailhead to Mount Shavano in 189 minutes. Mount Shavano to Tabeguache Peak in 48 minutes. Back to mount Shavano in 52 minutes. Mount Shavano to trailhead in 142 minutes. (Total 431 minutes)
Starting Elevation:	9,800 feet
Highest Elevation:	14,229 feet (4,337 meters)
Elevation Gain:	5,574 feet (includes 1,149 extra feet)
Difficulty:	More Difficult
Steepness Index:	0.17
Trail:	All the way except faint and intermittent up to Mount Shavano from each saddle.
Relevant Maps:	Trails Illustrated Number 130 Maysville 7½ minute Mount Antero 7½ minute Chaffee County Number Three San Isabel National Forest Colorado Trail Maps 14 and 15

Views from the Summit:

Mount Shavano
NNW to Mount Yale, Mount Harvard, Mount Columbia, Mount Antero, Mount Princeton and Mount White
NE to Jones Peak
ENE to Pikes Peak
ESE to Salida
SSE to Mount Ouray
SW to Mount Aetna
WNW to Tabeguache Peak

Tabeguache Peak
N to Mount White
NNW to Mount Yale, Mount Harvard, Mount Columbia and Mount Antero
ENE to Jones Peak
ESE to Mount Shavano
SSE to Mount Ouray
SW to Mount Aetna

Getting There: From the intersection of U.S. 24 and U.S. 285 south of Buena Vista, drive south on U.S. 285 for 20.1 miles and turn right onto Chaffee County Road 140. After 1.7 miles on this road, turn right onto Road 250. Stay on this main road and keep right at mile 3.6 and at mile 4.4. At mile 5.7 (from U.S. 285), take the left fork and again at mile 6.5 after crossing Placer Creek. Keep straight at mile 7.3 and left at mile 8.7. At mile 8.9 take the right fork and in another tenth of a mile park just below a stone memorial which honors L. Dale Hibbs who promoted Rocky Mountain Goat preservation. Regular cars can reach this point which was the former site of the Blank Cabin.

When hiking up fourteeners, there are two types of difficulty. There is the technical difficulty related to the care, dexterity and skill required in negotiating some of the rocky terrain. And there is also the stamina required. Length and elevation gain are important in this second category. These two fourteen-ers pose no technical difficulties in good weather but do require endurance.

The route uses a small segment of the Colorado Trail before ascending steeply to the west to reach a saddle and then the first summit. The second summit is a little more than a mile to the northwest via another saddle. This is only one of several ascent routes to these two high peaks.

From the memorial to L. Dale Hibbs, hike north northwest and take a quick right fork onto the Colorado Trail. After 0.3 miles turn left (west) onto the Mount Shavano Trail at a sign. Follow this good, steep trail through lovely forest. About halfway to timberline you hike parallel to a creek before ascending north to finally reach timberline after 3.0 miles from the trailhead. Continue west to a saddle with the snowy pattern, called the Angel of Shavano (by July, snow melt eliminates the outline), below to your left. Then turn north over a faint intermittent trail to reach the Mount Shavano summit easily. There are three poles amid boulders and a register cylinder at the top. If you want the second fourteener, descend northwest over gradual terrain and keep right of the ridge to a saddle and then up the ridge to Tabeguache Peak. The distance between summits is 1.1 mile. A rock shelter and register cylinder mark the high point. To return, retrace your ascent route and pass over the Mount Shavano summit. Trying to pass around and below this only makes the return route more difficult.

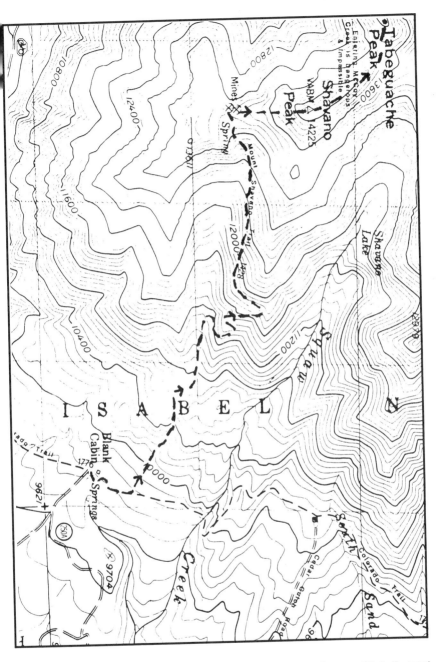

Courtesy of Trails Illustrated

31A Mount Bierstadt

Hike Distance:	4.1 miles each way
Hiking Time:	Up in 120 minutes. Down in 96 minutes.
Starting Elevation:	11,669 feet (Guanella Pass)
Highest Elevation:	14,060 feet (4,285 meters)
Elevation Gain:	2,761 feet (includes an extra 185 feet of elevation gain each way)
Difficulty:	Moderate
Steepness Index:	0.13
Trail:	All the way
Relevant Maps:	Mount Evans 7½ minute
	Clear Creek County
	Pike National Forest
	Trails Illustrated Number 104
Views from the Summit:	N to Gray Wolf Mountain
	NNE to Mount Spalding and the Sawtooth
	NNW to Grays Peak, Torreys Peak, and Mount Wilcox
	NE to Mount Evans
	SSE to Kataka Mountain
	SSW to South Park
	SE to Mount Logan
	WNW to Square Top Mountain

Getting There: Drive to Guanella Pass, either 11.0 miles south from the four-way stop signs in the middle of Georgetown (east of the town library) or 13.4 miles north from U.S. 285 at Grant via Park County Road 62 and park in the designated area on the east side of the pass. Regular cars can reach Guanella Pass from either the north or south.

Mount Bierstadt is named after Albert Bierstadt, the famous German painter of western U.S. scenery. The high trailhead and relatively short hiking distance make this one of the easier 14ers to hike.

From the parking area Mount Bierstadt can be seen to the east southeast with the Sawtooth, an impressive rock formation, to its left. The trail begins downward to the north northeast from the right side of the wooden Guanella Pass National Forest sign. The trail passes to the right of a small lake, crosses the creek and meanders northeast and then southeast through bushes. Take two consecutive left forks and follow the trail as it generally ascends, steeply at times, southeast to a notch to the right of the summit. It's mostly tundra above the bushes until you cross talus and boulders in your final ascent north from the notch. A register cylinder and a U.S.G.S. marker mark the summit. Descend on your ascent trail and thereby avoid bushwhacking and also help to perpetuate the trail for those to follow.

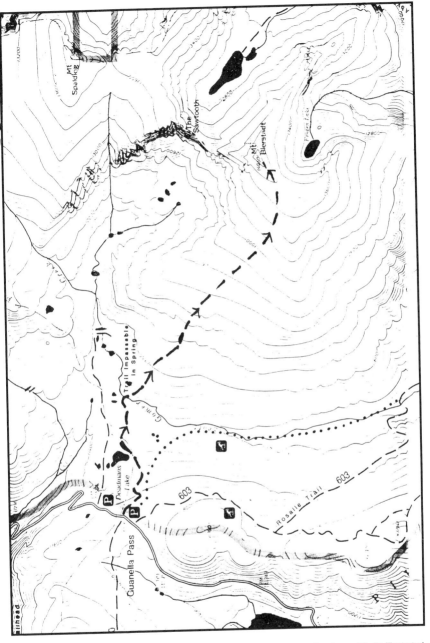

Courtesy of Trails Illustrated

133

31B Lawn Lake

Hike Distance:	6.2 miles each way
Hiking Time:	Up in 154 minutes. Down in 132 minutes.
Starting Elevation:	8,550 feet
Highest Elevation:	11,007 feet (3,355 meters)
Elevation Gain:	2,647 feet (includes 95 feet extra each way)
Difficulty:	Moderate
Steepness Index:	0.08
Trail:	All the way
Relevant Maps:	Trail Ridge 7½ minute
	Trails Illustrated Number 200
	Larimer County Number Three
	Rocky Mountain National Park

Getting There: Drive west on U.S. 34 for 2.1 miles from the Fall River Entrance to Rocky Mountain National Park and turn right and within 100 yards turn right again into a parking area at the Lawn Lake Trailhead.

When the dam broke in July, 1982, the waters of Lawn Lake swelled the Roaring River, widened its channnel, and spread death and destruction all the way to Estes Park. Since then, the dam has been rebuilt, Estes Park has had a renaissance, and the ecosystems of the ravaged area have begun to heal. However, on the hike to Lawn Lake you will still see considerable evidence of the flood.

Start your hike by ascending northeast from the trailhead sign. Within 75 yards take the left fork and within 100 yards farther take the right fork and continue on the excellent trail as it rises to the northwest to meet the Roaring River which will be on your left all the way to Lawn Lake. After 0.4 miles from the trailhead take a left fork, as a right fork just leads to an overlook. In 0.9 miles farther go right at a sign (the left fork leads to Chipmunk and Ypsilon Lakes). About a mile farther keep right at another fork. At 5.8 miles from the trailhead another fork and sign are reached. Take the left fork for the last 0.4 miles to Lawn Lake. A corral for horses lies on the southeast end of the lake and there is even a tether for llamas.

Campsites are available around the lake but require a backcountry permit. Mummy Mountain looms impressively to the north northwest, and Hagues Peak to the northwest. If you have the time and energy you may wish to hike to Crystal Lake and Little Crystal Lake and the pass known as The Saddle farther up the valley. The summits of Mummy Mountain, Hagues Peak, and Fairchild Mountain can all be reached from the valley above Lawn Lake.

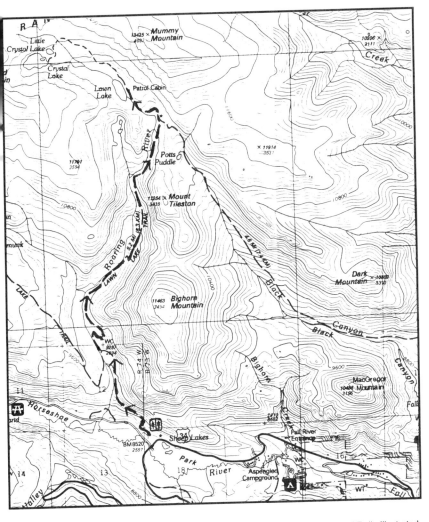

32A Shelf Lake

Hike Distance: 2.9 miles each way
Hiking Time: Up in 102 minutes. Down in 75 minutes.
Starting Elevation: 10,138 feet
Highest Elevation: 11,960 feet (3,645 meters)
Elevation Gain: 2,072 feet (includes 125 feet of extra elevation gain each
                    way)
Difficulty: Moderate
Steepness Index: 0.14
Trail: All the way
Relevant Maps: Montezuma 7½ minute
                    Trails Illustrated Number 104
                    Clear Creek County
                    Pike National Forest

Getting There: From Grant on U.S. 285, drive northwest on Park County Road 62 which leads to Guanella Pass and Georgetown. Follow Road 62 for 7.0 miles and turn left off the main road onto a road leading to Duck Creek Picnic Ground and Geneva Park Campground. (This cutoff is 6.4 miles south of Guanella Pass.) A sign marks this turnoff. Continue on this dirt road for 3.5 miles to a trailhead sign for Shelf Lake (Trail 634) on your right. Park around here off the road.

The Colorado mountains are full of nice surprises. Here is a good trail to a high lake which is relatively unknown. The views become inspiring as you arrive at timberline at the head of the gulch. Argentine Peak looms impressively to the north northeast of the lake as does Square Top Mountain to the east northeast. Decatur Mountain lies above and west of the lake.

For the hike, begin upward to the north northwest. In about 0.6 miles a series of five creek crossings begins. The last few can be demanding during the height of the spring runoff. The trail occasionally loses some altitude as you continue up through the trees. Near timberline the trail curves to your left (west) to reach Shelf Lake which will be partly frozen into July. This slightly used trail is ideal for those who like to hike along briskly flowing creeks.

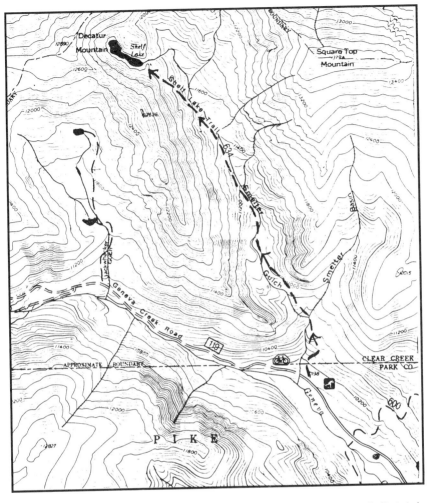

32B Mount Elbert

Hike Distance:	4.7 miles each way
Hiking Time:	Up in 180 minutes. Down in 130 minutes.
Starting Elevation:	10,075 feet
Highest Elevation:	14,433 feet (4,399 meters)
Elevation Gain:	4,448 feet (includes an extra 45 feet each way)
Difficulty:	More Difficult
Steepness Index:	0.18
Trail:	All the way
Relevant Maps:	Mount Massive 7½ minute
	Mount Elbert 7½ minute
	Trails Illustrated Number 127
	Lake County
	San Isabel National Forest

Views from the Summit: NNE to Turquoise Lake and Leadville
NNW to Mount of the Holy Cross
NW to Mount Massive
E to Twin Lakes
SSE to LaPlata Peak
SE to Mount Harvard and Mount Yale
W to French Mountain and Mount Sopris
WSW to Casco Peak, Pyramid Peak, The Maroon
Bells, Snowmass Mountain and Capitol Peak

Getting There: Drive south on U.S. 24 from the stoplight in Leadville at East 6th Street for 4.0 miles and turn right (west) onto Colorado 300. After 0.8 miles on Colorado 300 turn left onto unpaved Lake County Road 11. After 1.2 miles on this road turn right and follow this good dirt road past Halfmoon Campground for 5.5 more miles and park in the open area on the right. En route to this point take the left fork at mile 2.5 from Colorado 300. Regular cars can come this far.

Mount Elbert at 14,433 feet is the highest peak in Colorado. Only Mount Whitney in California is higher in the 48 contiguous United States. It is named after Samuel Elbert, a governor of the Colorado territories and a Colorado Supreme Court Judge in the 1870s and 1880s. This route is via the northeast ridge and, although steep, is the easiest and poses no special problems to the hiker. The middle third of this hike is the most difficult part due to its steepness.

Begin south at a trailhead sign and trail register. Continue up and down over several ridges and in 1.4 miles from the trailhead take the right fork in the trail. A sign states this fork is the trail to Mount Elbert. (The left fork descends and continues as the Colorado Trail.) Ascend into the trees and steeply rise to the southwest. In 1.5 miles from the fork you will reach timberline and be on the northeast ridge of Mount Elbert. Follow the steep but good trail over a false summit to gain the summit ridge. At the top there are a few rock shelters, a register cylinder and a nearby U.S.G.S. marker. The views are extraordinary. Return by your ascent route and be prepared for the steepness and loose rocks.

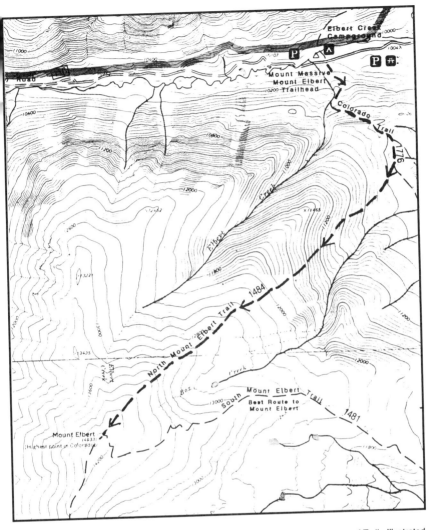

33A Bowen Pass

Hike Distance:	8.0 miles each way
Hiking Time:	Up in 196 minutes. Down in 150 minutes.
Starting Elevation:	8,810 feet
Highest Elevation:	11,476 feet (3,498 meters)
Elevation Gain:	2,906 feet (includes an extra 120 feet each way)
Difficulty:	Moderate
Steepness Index:	0.07
Trail:	All the way
Relevant Maps:	Grand Lake 7½ minute
	Bowen Mountain 7½ minute
	Trails Illustrated Number 200
	Grand County Number Two

Arapaho National Forest
Rocky Mountain National Park

Getting There: Drive via U.S. 34 north from Granby to the Grand Lake Entrance of Rocky Mountain National Park. Enter the park (fee required) and drive 6.3 miles to the Baker-Bowen Trailhead on the left and park in the paved designated area by the trailhead sign.

This lengthy hike to Bowen Pass begins in Rocky Mountain National Park, continues into the Arapaho National Forest and ends at the Continental Divide. This area is not heavily used and is very lush.

Begin west from the trailhead sign, cross a bridge, pass around a barrier to vehicles and traverse the lovely Kawuneeche Valley. After 0.2 miles, take two successive left forks and continue southwest. Pass a house on the right and cross a creek before entering the Arapaho National Forest at a sign board. 1.2 miles from the entry point into the National Forest, keep right as an old road enters from the left. In 0.2 miles farther you will reach a T. Take the right fork which leads west. In one mile from the T, cross the creek on a log and 0.2 miles farther cross the creek again and encounter a Never Summer Wilderness Area sign and a trail register. After another mile the trail turns back to the right and reaches a fork. Either fork is acceptable since the trails reconnect quickly. Take the left fork and soon pass a Bowen Gulch Trail Sign. In 0.8 miles from this sign you will reach a fork and a trail sign. The left fork goes to Bowen Lake. You take the right fork and ascend to timberline. Pass a large cairn as the trees become sparse and in 1.8 miles from the fork reach Bowen Pass at a pole in a cairn. You are now on the Continental Divide and the trail continues west down into the Routt National Forest. Ruby Peak lies along the ridge to your left (south) and Bowen Mountain looms above to the east.

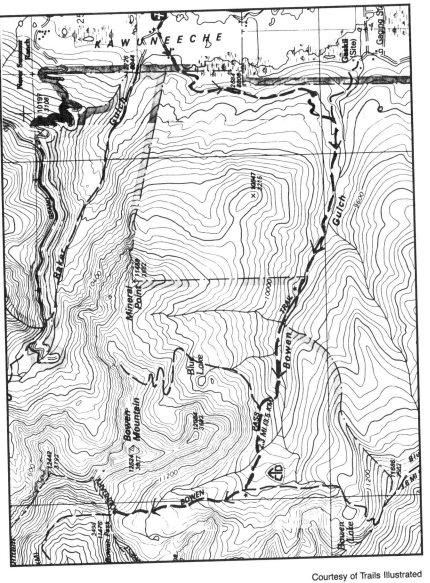

Courtesy of Trails Illustrated

33B Eaglesmere Lakes

Hike Distance:	4.0 miles each way.
Hiking Time:	Up in 118 minutes. Down in 90 minutes.
Starting Elevation:	8,720 feet
Highest Elevation:	10,397 feet (3,169 meters)
Elevation Gain:	1,861 feet (includes an extra 92 feet of gain each way)
Difficulty:	Moderate
Steepness Index:	0.09
Trail:	All the way
Relevant Maps:	Mount Powell 7½ minute
	Trails Illustrated Number 107
	Summit County Number One
	Arapaho National Forest

Getting There: From Interstate 70 at Silverthorne, drive northwest on Colorado 9 for 17.3 miles and turn left onto Summit County Road 30. After 5.6 miles on this road (with Green Mountain Reservoir to your right), turn left onto Summit County Road 1725 (the Cataract Lakes Road). After 1.3 miles on this road, take the left fork and 0.7 miles farther keep right and 0.1 miles farther take the right fork at the sign to Eaglesmere Trailhead. In 0.15 miles park at the trailhead as the road ends in a loop. Regular cars can readily reach this parking area.

This hike to the two Eaglesmere Lakes lies largely within the Gore Range Wilderness and uses some of the Gore Range Trail. The views from the trail are intermittent but lovely. There are extensive stands of aspen and grazing cows may leave some tokens over the lower part of the trail.

Begin west southwest from the trailhead sign, pass a trail register and pass through a fence. Soon you can see Lower Cataract Lake down to your left as you continue your ascent. The trail is clear but a bit eroded in spots. In 3.3 miles from the trailhead you will reach the Gore Range Trail going both left and to the right at some signs. Take the right fork and in a half mile reach another fork. Go left and in 0.2 more miles reach the two Eaglesmere Lakes. The lake to the south is the larger and Eagles Nest Peak looms over it impressively. Return by your ascent route after enjoying the tranquil beauty of these lakes.

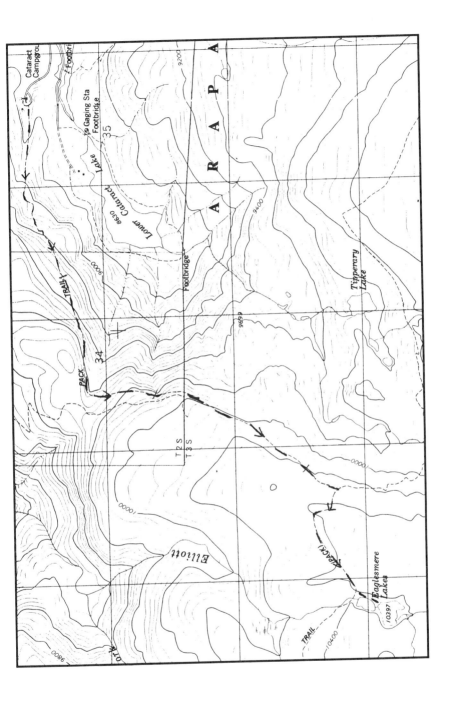

143

34A Eccles Pass

Hike Distance:	5.2 miles each way.
Hiking Time:	Up in 145 minutes. Down in 110 minutes.
Starting Elevation:	9,150 feet
Highest Elevation:	11,900 feet (3,627 meters)
Elevation Gain:	2,890 feet (includes 70 feet extra each way)
Difficulty:	Moderate
Steepness Index:	0.11
Trail:	All the way
Relevant Maps:	Frisco 7½ minute
	Vail Pass 7½ minute
	Trails Illustrated Number 108
	Summit County Number Two
	Arapaho National Forest (Dillon Ranger District)

Getting There: Take Exit 203 from Interstate 70 between Silverthorne and Frisco and drive west on the dirt road northwest of the bridge for 0.6 miles to the Meadow Creek Trailhead and parking area at the end of the road.

Here is a great hike in the Gore Range with easy access from Denver. The route follows Meadow Creek up a lovely valley and reaches Eccles Pass overlooking another gorgeous valley. The grade is gradual and you are not likely to encounter very many other hikers.

Start the hike by ascending northwest from the trailhead sign. In two minutes, take the left fork at a trail register. A half mile farther take another left fork at a sign. (The right fork goes to Lily Pad Lake.) After 1.4 miles from the trailhead you will make the first of three crossings of Meadow Creek. The second will occur 1.5 miles after the first and the third, which will not be assisted by a bridge, occurs 0.9 miles after the second. In 0.4 miles from the third crossing, the Gore Range Trail joins the trail from the left. From here it is one mile with some switchbacks to Eccles Pass which is marked by a wooden pole in a cairn. At the pass you can look over to the South Willow Creek drainage. Red Peak lies across the valley to the north northwest. Buffalo Mountain is northwest. Peak 1 and Tenmile Peak are southeast. The trail continues northwest and down into the next valley and will connect with the trail to Red Buffalo Pass and with the South Willow Creek Trail.

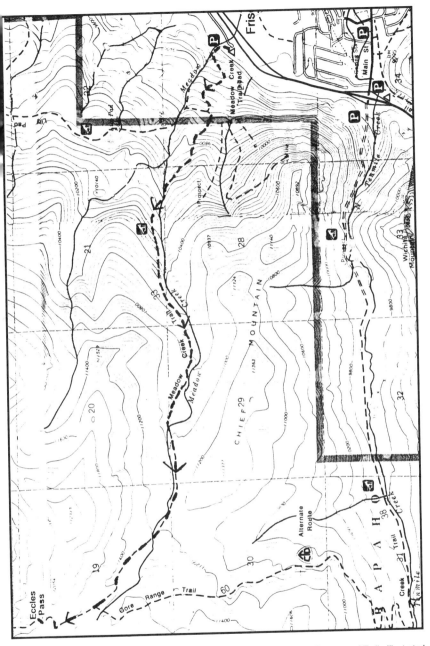

Courtesy of Trails Illustrated

34B Mount Audubon

Hike Distance: 3.7 miles each way.
Hiking Time: Up in 140 minutes. Down in 100 minutes.
Starting Elevation: 10,460 feet
Highest Elevation: 13,223 feet (4,030 meters)
Elevation Gain: 2,783 feet (includes an extra 20 feet due to trail undula-
                        tions)
Difficulty: Moderate
Steepness Index: 0.14
Trail: All the way
Relevant Maps: Ward 7½ minute
                        Trails Illustrated Number 102
                        Boulder County
                        Roosevelt National Forest
Views from the Summit: NNE to St. Vrain Mountain and Meadow Mountain
                        NNW to McHenrys Peak, Chiefs Head Peak, Pagoda
                        Mountain, Longs Peak and Mount Meeker
                        ESE to Mitchell Lake and Brainard Lake
                        SSW to Apache Peak
                        WSW to Mount Toll and Paiute Peak

Getting There: From the intersection of Colorado 72 and Colorado 119 in the center of Nederland, drive northwest on Colorado 72 for 12.0 miles and turn left at the Brainard Lake Recreation Area sign. Continue on this good paved road past the Pawnee Campground and over a bridge at the outlet of Brainard Lake and turn right after 5.3 miles from Colorado 72. Take a right fork in 0.1 mile farther and park at the trailhead as the road ends in a loop.

Named after ornithologist John James Audubon, this mountain lies in the Indian Peaks Wilderness. The trail is gradual, well-marked by cairns above the tundra and highly used in the hiking season. It's a good family hike if the children are over 10.

Begin northwest from the parking area on the Beaver Creek Trail and ascend through the trees. The trail turns northeast and becomes a bit steeper before reaching a sign at a fork 1.3 miles from the trailhead. Turn left and ascend west northwest. Within 0.3 miles you will pass the last scrub trees. The path loops around to the right to reach the final ascent ridge. Then follow the cairns to the south southwest to reach seven rock shelters around the other-wise unmarked summit. Return as you came up. By keeping on the trail, you diminish erosion and damage to plant life.

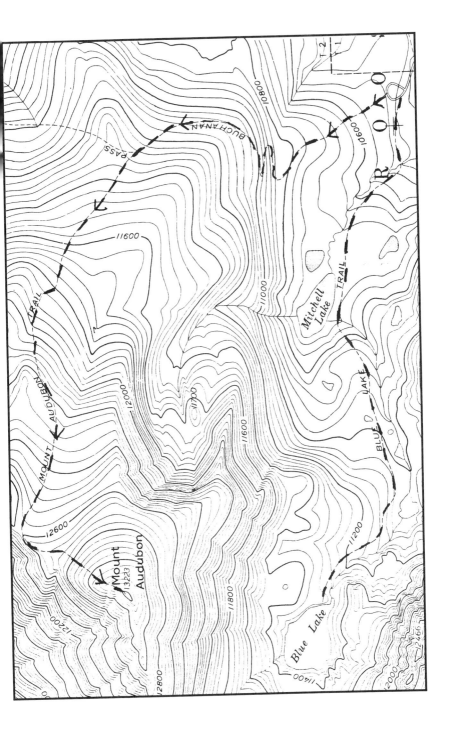

35A Mills Lake, Black Lake and Green Lake

Hike Distance: Trailhead to Mills Lake 2.5 miles. Mills Lake to Black Lake 2.0 miles. Black Lake to Green Lake 1.0 mile. (Total 5.5 miles)

Hiking Time: Up to Mills Lake in 50 minutes. 62 minutes more to Black Lake and 50 minutes more to Green Lake. (Total 162 minutes.) Down from Green Lake to Black Lake in 45 minutes. Black Lake to Mills Lake in 52 minutes. Mills Lake to trailhead in 46 minutes.

Starting Elevation: 9,210 feet

Highest Elevation: 11,545 feet (Green Lake) (3,519 meters)

Elevation Gain: 2,795 feet (total)

Difficulty: Moderate

Steepness Index: 0.10

Trail: Initial 90%

Relevant Maps: McHenrys Peak 7½ minute
Trails Illustrated Number 200
Larimer County Number Three
Boulder County
Rocky Mountain National Park

Getting There: From the Beaver Meadows Entrance Station to Rocky Mountain National Park (west of Estes Park), drive into the park for 0.2 miles and turn left onto the Bear Lake Road. Keep left after 1.3 miles more and follow the paved road for a total of 8.7 miles from the park entrance and park on the right at the Glacier Gorge Junction parking area.

Just two hours from Denver we have one of the premier national parks in the country. Rocky Mountain National Park has great facilities and trails, spread over vast, beautiful terrain. This hike takes you up Glacier Gorge into a breathtaking basin ringed by high peaks. The three destinations will enable you to select the length and elevation gain which suits you.

Begin south across the Bear Lake Road and ascend the trail to the southwest. Take the first left fork, continue south over a bridge and then take a right fork. After two more creek crossings, pass beautiful Alberta Falls on your left in about 0.3 miles from the trailhead. Continue up the rocky trail marked with occasional cairns and in 0.6 more miles take the right fork at a sign. After 0.4 miles at another sign take the left trail toward Mills Lake. (The right trail goes to Loch Vale.) Cross two bridges within the next 0.4 miles and soon thereafter emerge at Mills Lake. Longs Peak will be visible to the southeast with Pagoda Mountain the next peak to the right. The trail continues along the east (left) side of Mills Lake and up to Black Lake with Glacier Creek always to your right. The abundance of flowing water makes this hike especially pleasant. From Black Lake ascend east northeast on a good trail which gradually curves to the south after you have reached the bench above Black Lake. Continue directly south with the aid of a series of cairns as the trail gradually ends in tundra. With Longs Peak above you to the left and the dramatic Spearhead to the right, continue south along the creek to reach the aptly named Green Lake. Pagoda Mountain rises to the southeast and Chiefs Head Peak and a glacier to the south. The rock formations here are dramatic. You may choose to explore nearby Frozen Lake a half mile to the west or Blue Lake to your north northeast as you return to Black Lake.

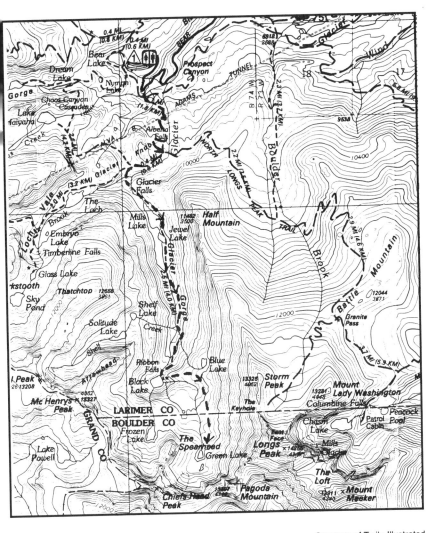

Courtesy of Trails Illustrated

35B Kit Carson Peak and Obstruction Peak

Hike Distance:	9.7 miles each way. Day 1: 5.3 miles. Day 2: 14.1 miles.
Hiking Time:	Day 1: 150 minutes to base camp. Day 2: Up in 310 minutes. Down to base camp in 260 minutes. Base camp to car in 135 minutes.
Starting Elevation:	8,720 feet
Highest Elevation:	14,165 feet (4,317 meters)
Elevation Gain:	7,625 feet. Day 1: 2,480 feet. Day 2: 5,145 feet (includes 2,180 extra feet)
Difficulty:	Most Difficult
Steepness Index:	0.15
Trail:	From trailhead to Upper South Colony Lake. From saddle east of Obstruction Peak to Kit Carson Peak.

149

Relevant Maps: Beck Mountain 7½ minute
                  Crestone Peak 7½ minute
                  Custer County Number One
                  Saguache County Number Five
                  San Isabel National Forest
Views from the Summit:

Obstruction Peak
NNW to Mount Adams and Horn Peak
NE to Colony Baldy
E to Humboldt Peak
SE to Crestone Needle and Crestone Peak
W to Kit Carson Peak

Kit Carson Peak
N to Horn Peak
NNW to Mt. Adams
NE to Colony Baldy
E to Humboldt Peak and Obstruction Peak
SE to Crestone Needle and Crestone Peak
W to Challenger Point

Getting There: From the intersection of Colorado 69 and Colorado 96 in Westcliffe, drive south on Colorado 96 for 4.6 miles and turn right onto Colfax Lane. Keep straight on Colfax Lane for 5.6 miles to a T. Turn right onto Road 120 and park on the right after 1.5 miles on this road. (Four-wheel drive vehicles can negotiate this very rough road 5.3 miles farther west to the South Colony Lakes Trailhead. This would save the distance and elevation gain of Day 1.)

This is a very demanding two-day hike but the rewards are great. The South Colony Lakes are surrounded by three visible fourteeners and a fourth, Kit Carson Peak, lies just out of view to the west. This basin is one of the premier scenic areas in the state. This area is popular not only with hikers but also campers and fishermen. There are three ways to lessen the difficulty of this hike as described. Use a four-wheel drive vehicle with high clearance up to the South Colony Lakes trailhead, make the lakes your destination or take three days instead of two. Humboldt Peak is the easiest fourteener to ascend from this basin.

Begin hiking west up the rough road which eventually bends to the southwest, crosses the Rainbow Trail and South Colony Creek before finally arriving in 5.3 miles at a sign on the right for the South Colony Lakes Trail. Continue west on this trail, leave the road and find a campsite. This ends day one. On day two continue west up the valley past the Lower and Upper South Colony Lakes by trail. Be careful not to get caught in the willows near the lower lake. If possible keep to the right and above them to regain the trail as it continues to the upper lake. Follow the trail around Upper South Colony Lake to the left and continue west up into the basin as the trail fades away. Pick your way among several possibilities up to the ridge which overlooks a large grassy area descending to the left. This is called the Bears Playground. Losing as little elevation as possible, angle diagonally to the west to gain the saddle at 13,500 feet to the west of unnamed Peak 13,799. At this saddle you have come 3.4 miles from your campsite. Continue west up the prominent subpeak of Obstruction Peak by a trail along the south edge of the ridge. At the top of this subpeak Kit Carson Peak will now be visible. Continue west another few hundred yards to the top of Obstruction Peak with a register cylinder. The most difficult part of this hike is now the four hundred foot descent by cairns to the west. A series of ledges and couloirs descend to a saddle. A dramatic rock cut to the north is avoided by descending to its left. From the saddle it is an easy ascent to the west by trail and cairns to the top of Kit Carson Peak. On my recent hike, there were no markers or registers at the high point. Challenger Point, a newly named fourteener, can be seen to the west but involves a serious descent to another saddle. I recommend you climb Challenger Point from a Willow Lakes base camp. The keys to your return will be to find the route you used coming down Obstruction Peak. Hopefully you have allowed for enough daylight, because your return is a lengthy one.

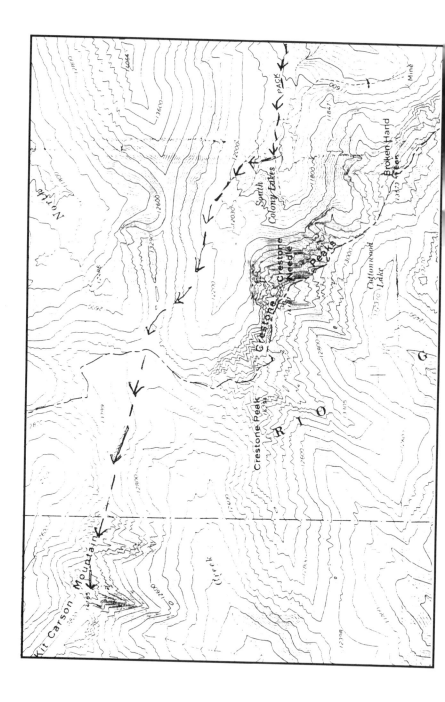

36A Mount Irving Hale 11,754 feet

Hike Distance:	6.1 miles each way.
Hiking Time:	Up in 170 minutes. Down in 125 minutes.
Starting Elevation:	8,300 feet
Highest Elevation:	11,754 feet (3,583 meters)
Elevation Gain:	3,634 feet (includes 90 extra feet each way)
Difficulty:	Moderate
Steepness Index:	0.11
Trail:	All the way to the Hale Divide. Intermittent trail thereafter.
Relevant Maps:	Isolation Peak 7½ minute
	Shadow Mountain 7½ minute
	Trails Illustrated Number 102
	Grand County Number Two
	Arapaho National Forest
Views from the Summit:	N to Watanga Mountain
	NE to Crawford Lake, Hiamovi Mountain, Ogalalla Peak and Elk Tooth
	NW to Twin Peaks
	ESE to Long Lake
	SE to Paiute Peak
	W to Lake Granby

Getting There: From the intersection with U.S. 40 west of Granby, drive north on U.S. 34 for 5.4 miles and turn right. Follow this good dirt road around the southeastern edge of Lake Granby for a total of 9.7 miles from U.S. 34 and park at the designated area on the right for the Roaring Fork Trail. En route to this point go left at mile 1.2, right at mile 1.4 and left at mile 8.8 and drive through the campground. Regular cars will have no trouble reaching the parking area.

Colonel Irving Hale was Colorado's first graduate from the U.S. Military Academy at West Point, New York. Camp Hale, northwest of Leadville, and the peak at the terminus of this hike are named in his honor.

This route uses the little used Roaring Fork Trail to a saddle, known as the Hale Divide, and then a direct off-trail ascent of the ridge to the south.

Enter the trees to the north from the parking area and within a few hundred yards take a right fork and pass a trail sign. Then ascend some steep switch-backs before the trail parallels the aptly named Roaring Fork and arrives after 1.2 miles at a trail intersection. Go to the right and immediately cross the Roaring Fork on a two log bridge. Continue up along the creek for 1.6 more miles before crossing a side creek and quickly arriving at another fork. Pro-ceed to the right and within 100 yards cross another two log bridges. Keep left as your trail joins a trail entering from the right and very quickly reach a trail sign at a fork. Watanga Lake is reached by the left fork and you continue right (east) on the Roaring Fork Trail. In 1.8 more steep miles you will arrive at the saddle, known as the Hale Divide. The vista from this area is magni-ficent. Mount Irving Hale will now be visible to the south. Leave the trail, cross tundra and later boulders, passing to the right of a subpeak to reach the rocky high point which is only marked by a few rocks on a summit boulder. Some easy hand work is needed just below the summit. The views are

special in every direction especially down into Hell Canyon to the east. Return
to the saddle and the trail for your descent.

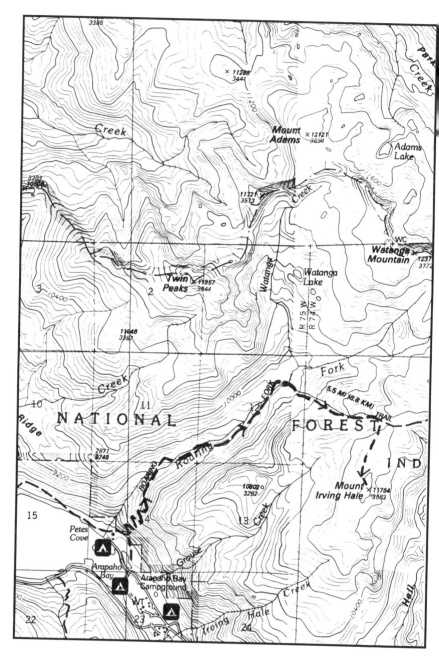

36B Grizzly Lake

Hike Distance:	3.8 miles each way.
Hiking Time:	Up in 112 minutes. Down in 96 minutes.
Starting Elevation:	10,570 feet
Highest Elevation:	12,520 feet (3,816 meters)
Elevation Gain:	2,058 feet (includes an extra 108 feet)
Difficulty:	Moderate
Steepness Index:	0.10
Trail:	All the way
Relevant Maps:	Independence Pass 7½ minute
	New York Peak 7½ minute
	Trails Illustrated Number 127
	Pitkin County Number Two
	White River National Forest

Getting There: Drive on Colorado 82 for 11.3 miles west of Independence Pass or for 9.2 miles east of the Aspen town limits and turn south onto the Lincoln Creek Road. Keep left at 0.4 miles and again at 3.2 miles from Colorado 82. Stay on the main road and reach Grizzly Reservoir on your right at mile 6.1. Continue south and in 0.1 mile farther take the left fork toward the Portal Campground. In 0.2 miles more you will pass the Grizzly Lake Trailhead, hidden in the trees on your left. Drive 100 feet farther and take a left fork and park off the road just after the intersection. The Lincoln Creek Road is unpaved and rough in spots but can be negotiated by regular cars with adequate clearance.

Here is a hike near Aspen which is somewhat off the beaten path. It passes upward along a creek through a lovely gulch with a ridge of the Continental Divide above to your left and imposing Grizzly Peak to the south southwest. There are many lakes, creeks and mountains in Colorado named Grizzly.

Begin east from a trail register and sign and rise through the trees to reach a lovely open area. Pass a cabin ruin on your left after 2.0 miles. Continue south and eventually cross Grizzly Creek at 11,430 feet. The trail rises above timberline and curves to the southwest to reach Grizzly Lake below the imposing flanks of Grizzly Peak. The final ascent involves a narrow segment along the side of a cliff just below the lake.

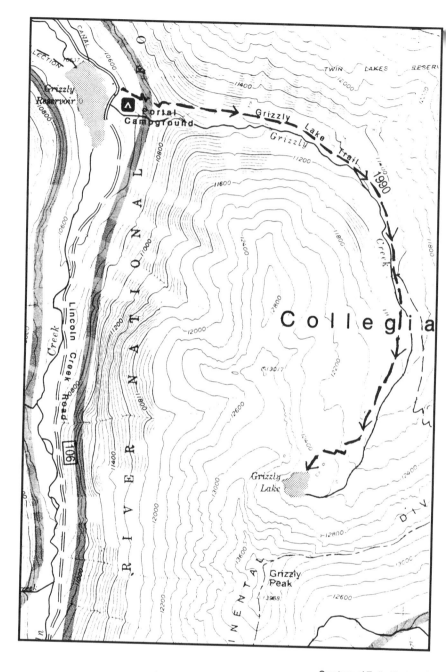

Courtesy of Trails Illustrated

37A Parika Lake 11,380 feet and Baker Pass 11,253 feet

Hike Distance:	5.2 miles to Parika Lake. 2.0 miles to Baker Pass. 6.2 miles down from Baker Pass. (Total Loop: 13.4 miles)
Hiking Time:	168 minutes to Parika Lake. 57 minutes over to Baker Pass, and 137 minutes down from Baker Pass. (Total 362 minutes)
Starting Elevation:	8,850 feet
Highest Elevation:	11,386 feet (3,470 meters)
Elevation Gain:	3,106 feet (includes 570 extra feet)
Difficulty:	Moderate
Steepness Index:	0.08
Trail:	All the way
Relevant Maps:	Grand Lake 7½ minute
	Bowen Mountain 7½ minute
	Mount Richthofen 7½ minute
	Trails Illustrated Number 200
	Grand County Number Two
	Arapaho National Forest

Getting There: From the western entrance to Rocky Mountain National Park (northwest of Grand Lake), drive north on Trail Ridge Road (U.S. 34) for 6.3 miles and park in the area on the left at the Baker-Bowen Trailhead.

Few hikes have as many positives as this one. The trail is excellent through gorgeous country; motor vehicles are forbidden; the trail is used by relatively few hikers and there is plenty of flowing water along the way.

Since the trailhead is located within Rocky Mountain National Park, an entrance fee is required. Most of this hike however lies in the Never Summer Wilderness Area of the Arapaho National Forest.

Begin west from the parking area and cross the Kawuneeche Valley. As the trail enters the trees, it forks at a sign. Go right (west) and ascend Baker Gulch. Soon pass a trail register at the wilderness sign and continue up the valley. Eventually traverse a talus slope. After 3.7 miles from the parking area, the trail joins a road along the Grand Ditch. Go left and quickly cross the ditch on a bridge. In 0.3 miles farther you will reach a fork and trail sign just past a creek crossing. Take the left fork and ascend more steeply to another fork and trail sign in one more mile. Take the left fork and reach secluded Parika Lake in 0.2 miles farther. (The trail continues south southwest to the left of the lake.) After a respite at the lake, return 0.2 miles to the fork and go left (north) toward the Baker Trail. This good trail rises and falls for 2.0 miles before reaching wide, flat Baker Pass which is marked by two separate poles in cairns. This pass is on the Continental Divide. To return follow the cairns south down the gulch until the trail resumes and returns you to the trail intersection where you originally went left toward Parika Lake. Go left here and return to the trailhead.

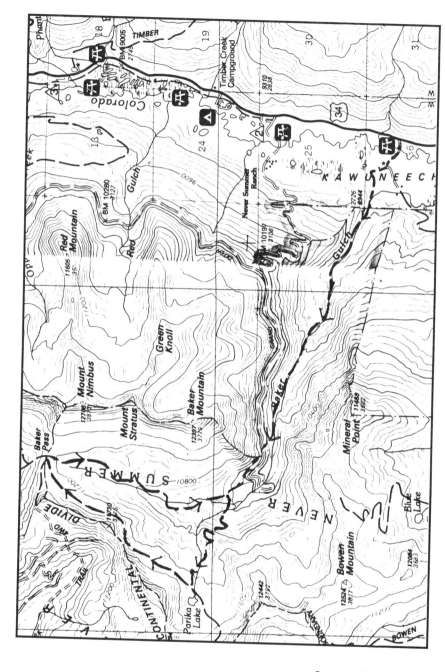

Courtesy of Trails Illustrated

37B Littlejohn's Cabins

Hike Distance:	6.6 miles each way
Hiking Time:	Up in 157 minutes. Down in 132 minutes.
Starting Elevation:	8,960 feet
Highest Elevation:	10,710 feet (3,264 meters)
Elevation Gain:	1,890 feet (includes an extra 70 feet each way)
Difficulty:	Moderate
Steepness Index:	0.05
Trail:	All the way
Relevant Maps:	Harvard Lakes 7½ minute
	Mount Harvard 7½ minute
	Trails Illustrated Number 129
	Chaffee County Number One
	San Isabel National Forest

Getting There: Drive on U.S. 24 to Chaffee County Road 388 leading southwest. This intersection is 6.4 miles south of the intersection of U.S. 24 with Colorado 82 or 13.3 miles north of the stoplight at Main Street in Buena Vista. On Chaffee Road 388 keep left after 0.3 miles and right after 0.3 miles farther. Park around here since the dirt road now becomes quite rough.

The trail leading southwest along Pine Creek takes you into a beautiful valley in the Collegiate Peaks Wilderness. Four fourteeners and several other high peaks and lakes can be reached from this valley and flowing water is abundant throughout the hike.

Harry Littlejohn's cabins were built around 1881 and are listed in the National Registry of Historic Landmarks. A trail to the Mount Harvard summit begins from the forge and burro shed across the creek on the southern edge of Littlejohn's land.

Begin south from your parking area past a trail sign and a gate which blocks the road to cars. Follow the good trail and in 1.5 miles reach a trail register. The trail soons gets steeper. Go right at a fork keeping Pine Creek to your right. The trail gets narrow in spots with some steep drop-offs down to Pine Creek. Pass a wilderness sign and in 4.3 miles from the trailhead reach a bridge and an intersection with the Colorado Trail. Cross the bridge and continue west up the valley with Pine Creek now on your left. Soon a fork is reached with a Colorado Trail sign. Go left. 1.9 miles after the bridge crossing, the trail passes through a collapsed fence and in 0.4 miles more reaches Littlejohn's abandoned cabins in an enclosure. The Pine Creek Trail continues to ascend southwest past Bedrock Falls into beautiful Missouri Basin and then forks with the left trail leading to Silver King Lake and the right to Elkhead Pass. These destinations each are more than five miles past Littlejohn's cabins. Retrace your ascent route to return.

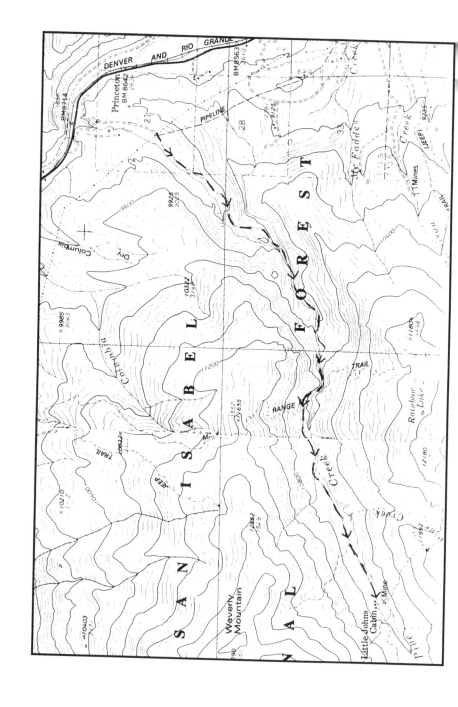

160

38A Mitchell Lake and Blue Lake

Hike Distance:	2.8 miles each way
Hiking Time:	Up in 66 minutes. Down in 60 minutes.
Starting Elevation:	10,460 feet
Highest Elevation:	11,300 feet (3,444 meters)
Elevation Gain:	1,000 feet (includes an extra 80 feet each way)
Difficulty:	Easy
Steepness Index:	0.07
Trail:	All the way
Relevant Maps:	Ward 7½ minute
	Trails Illustrated Number 102
	Boulder County
	Roosevelt National Forest

Getting There: Drive northwest from Nederland on Colorado 72 for 11.7 miles and turn left onto the Brainard Lake Road. Continue for 5.7 miles on this paved road to the Mitchell Lake Trailhead. En route keep right at mile 5.2 and at mile 5.3. Park in the large designated area.

Of the many lakes called Blue Lake in Colorado, this one in the Indian Peaks Wilderness is my nominee for most scenic. After passing lovely Mitchell Lake, the trail crosses much flowing water before arriving at Blue Lake which lies at timberline in a bowl encircled by four of the Indian Peaks: Pawnee Peak, Mount Toll, Paiute Peak and Mount Audubon. This is a very popular hiking area and excellent for families.

Start hiking to the southwest from the Mitchell Lake Trailhead. Cross a bridge after 0.4 miles and pass a wilderness sign. After 1.0 mile from the trailhead Mitchell Lake will appear on your right. Take some time to explore this lake and the vistas to the west. Resume toward Blue Lake and soon cross a creek on logs, pass some small unnnamed ponds, finally ascend to timberline on the excellent trail and reach scenic Blue Lake. Pawnee Peak lies above to the south southwest (left), Mount Toll to the west southwest, Paiute Peak to the west northwest and Mount Audubon to the northwest (right).

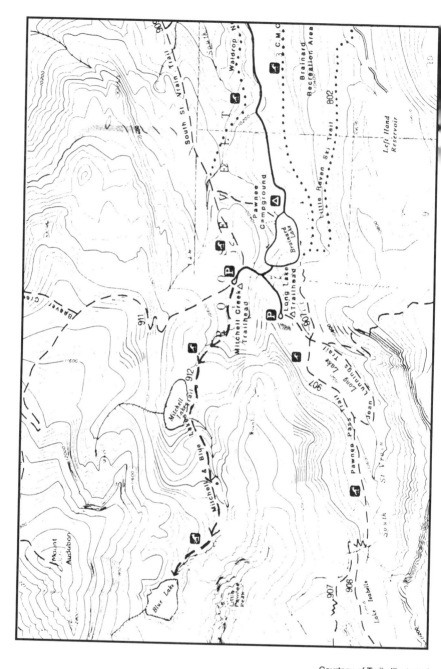

Courtesy of Trails Illustrated

38B Finch Lake and Pear Reservoir

Hike Distance:	4.6 miles to Finch Lake. 2.0 miles farther to Pear Reservoir. (Total 6.6 miles)
Hiking Time:	To Finch Lake in 135 minutes. 67 minutes farther to Pear Reservoir. Down in 159 minutes.
Starting Elevation:	8,475 feet
Highest Elevation:	10,582 feet (3,225 meters)
Elevation Gain:	2,781 feet (includes 337 extra feet each way)
Difficulty:	Moderate
Steepness Index:	0.08
Trail:	All the way
Relevant Maps:	Allens Park 7½ minute
	Trails Illustrated Number 200
	Boulder County
	Roosevelt National Forest
	Rocky Mountain National Park

Getting There: From the west end of Lyons, drive south and west on Colorado 7 for 20.7 miles and turn left into the Wild Basin area. After 0.4 miles, turn right and follow the good dirt road toward the Wild Basin Ranger Station for 2.2 miles and park on the left at the Finch Lake Trailhead. The entire road to the Ranger Station is easily negotiated by regular cars.

Here is a Rocky Mountain National Park hike which takes you to two lovely bodies of water and requires no park fee. Pets, bicylces and guns are forbidden on all trails within the park.

Start hiking south southeast from the trailhead sign and soon ascend to the east. The excellent trail will curve right (south) when you reach the top of a ridge. After 1.4 miles from the trailhead, reach a four-way intersection and a sign. Take the right fork and continue up to the west. In 1.0 mile farther reach a second four-way intersection and trail signs at the top of another ridge. Continue straight and soon pass through a stand of burnt trees. Longs Peak and the adjacent mountains will be visible to your right (northwest). After the burnt area, eventually cross a creek and then descend to Finch Lake on your left. From the lake bald Saint Vrain Mountain lies to the south southeast and Copeland Mountain to the west southwest. Continue around to the right of the lake and pass two campgrounds. (A backcountry permit is required to camp.) Continue up southwest and in 0.2 miles cross Cony Creek, later pass a small unnamed lake through the trees to your left, ascend more steeply and then cross Pear Creek. Turn right at a sign (a campground is to the left) and follow the trail until it ends near a corral at Pear Reservoir. The reservoir lies at the foot of rugged Copeland Mountain to the west and the impressive peak to the southwest is the Elk Tooth. On your way back down, Meadow Mountain is visible to the east and Saint Vrain Mountain to the east southeast.

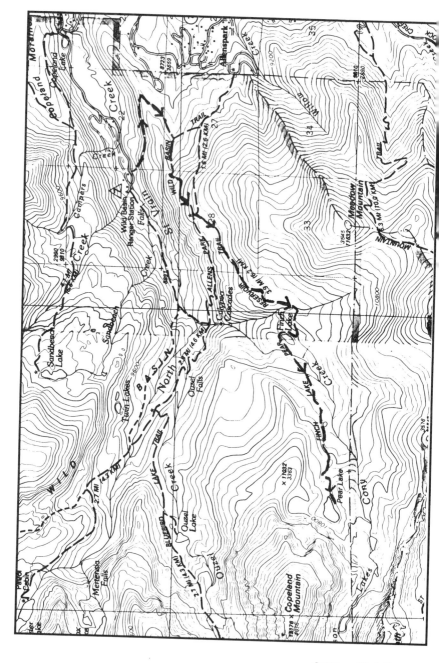

Courtesy of Trails Illustrated

164

39A Mount Chapin

Hike Distance:	1.8 miles each way
Hiking Time:	Up in 65 minutes. Down in 55 minutes.
Starting Elevation:	11,025 feet
Highest Elevation:	12,454 feet (3,796 meters)
Elevation Gain:	1,489 feet (includes an extra 30 feet each way)
Difficulty:	Easy
Steepness Index:	0.16
Trail:	First half
Relevant Maps:	Trail Ridge 7½ minute
	Trails Illustrated Number 200
	Larimer County Number Three
	Rocky Mountain National Park
Views from the Summit:	NNE to Hagues Peak
	NE to Mount Chiquita
	SSE to McHenrys Peak
	SE to Twin Sisters Peaks, the Estes Cone, Mount Meeker, Longs Peak, Pagoda Mountain and Chiefs Head Peak
	W to Mount Richthofen

Getting There: From the northwestern edge of Estes Park, enter Rocky Mountain National Park by the Fall River Entrance and drive 2.1 miles west on U.S. 34 and then turn right into Horseshoe Park. Follow this road up the valley where it becomes Fall River Road which is a good one-way dirt road leading up to the Alpine Visitor Center at Fall River Pass and Trail Ridge Road. Ascend scenic Fall River Road for 8.6 miles from U.S. 34 and park off the road on the left at the Chapin Pass Trailhead which is on the right side of the road.

Fall River Road is one of the many treasures of Rocky Mountain National Park. The rushing waters of Fall River can be seen on the left as you ascend this one-way road up a steep canyon to connect with Trail Ridge Road. The road is open from late June until October. Regular cars can traverse this excellent dirt road. A descriptive booklet with information about the Fall River Road can be purchased at park visitor centers. Mount Chapin is the most southerly peak of the Mummy Range.

Begin steeply to the north from the trailhead sign. In a few hundred yards reach unmarked Chapin Pass at 11,150 feet. Take a right fork here at a sign which describes the Mount Chapin Trail. Continue southeast and eventually pass a small tarn on your right just below timberline. Take a right fork just past the tarn and ascend the trail to the east past the last trees. The green rounded hill to the north is a false summit of Mount Chapin. Continue east toward the right side of the saddle between Mount Chiquita and Mount Chapin. Do not lose any elevation and keep your ascent gradual as the trail ends and you walk over tundra and some talus to a cairn and a few rock shelters atop Mount Chapin. Enjoy the magnificent views in every direction. A false summit can be seen to the southwest. An option from this point is to walk the ridge to the northeast to Mount Chiquita and Mount Ypsilon, both over 13,000 feet. Return by generally retracing your ascent route back to the trail.

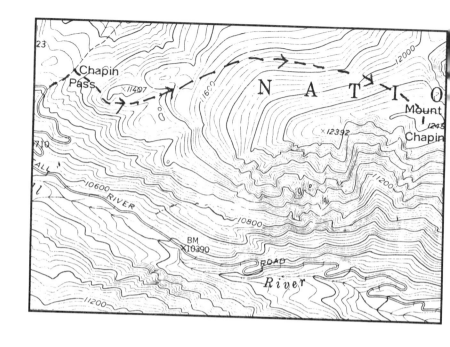

39B Silver Dollar Lake and Murray Lake

Hike Distance:	2.0 miles each way
Hiking Time:	Up is 66 minutes. Down in 48 minutes.
Starting Elevation:	11,160 feet
Highest Elevation:	12,336 feet (3,760 meters)
Elevation Gain:	1,342 feet (includes an extra 65 feet each way)
Difficulty:	Easy
Steepness Index:	0.12
Trail:	All the way except the last 100 yards
Relevant Maps:	Mount Evans 7½ minute
	Montezuma 7½ minute
	Trails Illustrated Number 104
	Clear Creek County
	Arapaho National Forest

Getting There: From the four-way intersection with stop signs in the center of Georgetown, drive south on the road to Guanella Pass for 8.9 miles and turn right. Drive up the steep dirt road for 0.6 miles and park in the designated area on the right. Most regular cars can reach this point.

The beauty of Silver Dollar and Murray Lakes draws many hikers. The trail quickly passes timberline south of Naylor Lake (on open private property), continues west to Silver Dollar Lake and rises over tundra to isolated Murray Lake with Mount Wilcox looming above to the north, Argentine Peak to the west and Square Top Mountain to the south southeast.

Begin hiking south southwest from the trail sign and in 0.8 miles reach timberline. The vistas from here onward are lovely and Naylor Lake lies below to the north. Continue west and in 1.6 miles from the trailhead reach Silver Dollar Lake on the left. Continue southwest up the trail which then curves north and leads you directly in 0.4 miles to secluded Murray Lake which drains into Naylor Lake. The Continental Divide is an easy mile to the west if you wish to explore further.

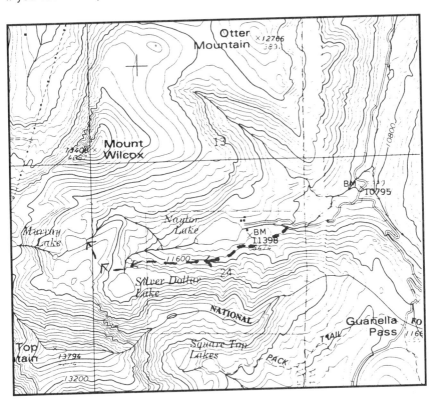

40A Ptarmigan Peak (Summit County)

Hike Distance:	5.3 miles each way
Hiking Time:	Up is 170 minutes. Down in 110 minutes.
Starting Elevation:	9,050 feet
Highest Elevation:	12,498 feet (3,809 meters)
Elevation Gain:	3,548 feet (includes 50 extra feet each way)
Difficulty:	More Difficult
Steepness Index:	0.13
Trail:	All the way
Relevant Maps:	Dillon 7½ minute
	Trails Illustrated Number 108
	Summit County Number Two
	Arapaho National Forest—Dillon Ranger District
Views from the Summit:	NW to Ute Peak
	E to Torreys Peak and Grays Peak
	S to Quandary Peak

SSW to Peak One
SE to Mount Guyot and Bald Mountain
SW to Buffalo Mountain and Red Peak

Getting There: Take Exit 205 from Interstate 70 and drive north a few hundred yards on Colorado 9 and turn right at the stoplight onto Tanglewood Drive. After 0.3 miles from Colorado 9 turn right onto County Road 2021. After another 0.3 miles on this road, keep straight at a fork and after 0.5 miles from the fork park in the designated area on the right. (You will have driven 0.8 miles on County Road 2021 and a total of 1.1 miles from Colorado 9.) Regular cars will have no trouble reaching the trailhead parking area.

The new trailhead for Ptarmigan Peak, one of the Williams Fork Mountains, is now open. In the past there were some access problems due to private property. This is a good trail with considerable elevation gain. The only flowing water along the way is a small creek at about the middle of the hike. The hiker will be rewarded with lovely forest and wonderful views, especially of Lake Dillon and the Gore Range.

Start your hike across the road to the north. Be careful to stay on the trail for the first half mile since you are crossing private property. After a few hundred yards from the trailhead continue up and straight (north) at a four-way intersection. Don't be deterrred by the "Private Road — No Access" sign. Pass this sign, intended for vehicles, and in about 50 feet follow the trail to the right off the road at a sign. Ascend steeply and stay on the main trail as it proceeds generally to the north. Keep right at three successive forks in the next few hundred yards and arrive at a four-way intersection. Continue straight under the power lines and enter the trees to the north. Follow the good trail then as it ascends Ptarmigan Peak and several aspen groves with some switchbacks before timberline. Continue north past the last trees for a final mile on a faint road with an occasional cairn to mark the trail. The summit is marked by a pole in a cairn. The views from here are excellent, so bring a camera. Return by your ascent route.

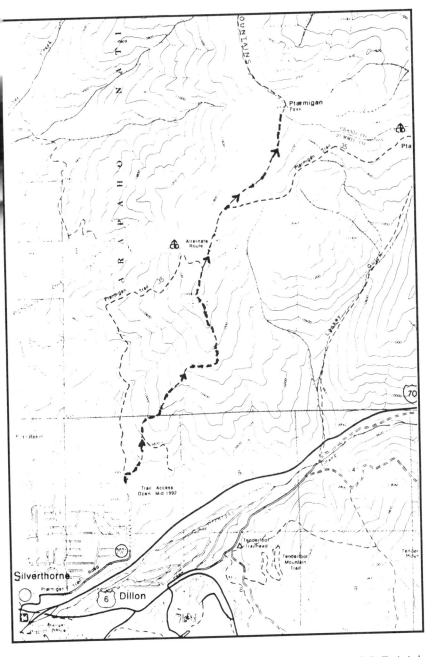

Courtesy of Trails Illustrated

169

40B Timber Lake

Hike Distance:	5.1 miles each way
Hiking Time:	Up in 150 minutes. Down in 115 minutes.
Starting Elevation:	9,100 feet
Highest Elevation:	11,040 feet (3,365 meters)
Elevation Gain:	2,110 feet (includes an extra 85 feet each way)
Difficulty:	Moderate
Steepness Index:	0.08
Trail:	All the way
Relevant Maps:	Fall River Pass 7½ minute
	Grand Lake 7½ minute
	Trails Illustrated Number 200
	Grand County Number Two
	Rocky Mountain National Park

Getting There: Drive on U.S. 34 either via Trail Ridge Road in Rocky Mountain National Park or Grand Lake. The Timber Lake trailhead parking area is on the east side of the road 11.0 miles south from the Alpine Visitor Center on Trail Ridge Road or 9.2 miles north from the Grand Lake Entrance to Rocky Mountain National Park. The national park requires an entrance fee.

The west side of Rocky Mountain National Park receives fewer visitors than the eastern part but is equally magnificent. The trail to Timber Lake is gradual, well-marked and ends in a beautiful basin near timberline. There are several campgrounds accessible from the trail.

Begin north northeast from the parking area and signs on the clear trail. Lose some elevation and in a half mile cross a creek. After another 0.8 miles, take a left fork and proceed east northeast. In 1.8 miles more, after another creek crossing, take another left fork leading to the west. Timber Creek soon will appear on your right along with some trail signs. Continue left as the trail gets steeper. Avoid the side trails to campgrounds and eventually pass through a small meadow and follow the trail as it bends to the east to finally gain Timber Lake surrounded on three sides by rocky peaks. Mount Ida lies to the east. The recommended way back to the parking area is by your ascent route.

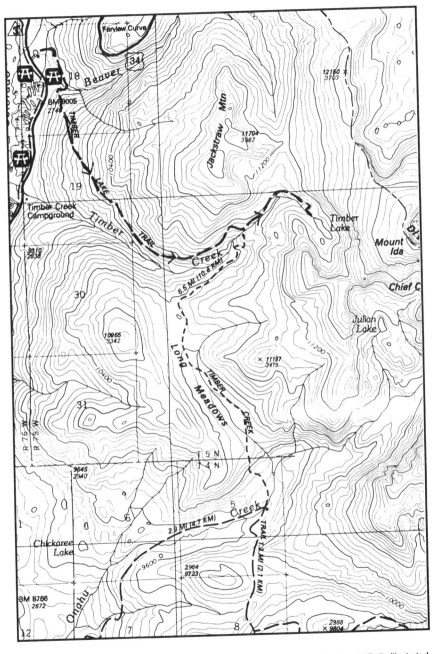

41A Blue Lake (Larimer County)

Hike Distance:	5.0 miles each way
Hiking Time:	Up in 112 minutes. Down in 88 minutes.
Starting Elevation:	9,500 feet
Highest Elevation:	10,805 feet (3,293 meters)
Elevation Gain:	1,605 feet (includes an extra 150 feet each way)
Difficulty:	Moderate
Steepness Index:	0.06
Trail:	All the way
Relevant Maps:	Chambers Lake 7½ minute
	Clark Peak 7½ minute
	Trails Illustrated Number 112
	Larimer County Number Three
	Roosevelt National Forest

Getting There: Drive west on Colorado 14 from its junction with U.S. 287 northwest of Fort Collins for 53.1 miles up Poudre Canyon. Park on the right at the Blue Lake Trailhead.

Many Coloradans never visit the Rawah Wilderness. This is a wild, out-of-the-way area which is full of lakes, trails and twelve thousand foot peaks. Here is a hike to introduce you to this wonderful playground. This lake is one of many in Colorado called Blue Lake.

Start hiking west northwest from the trailhead sign. The trail is clear and marked at intervals by blue diamond signs on the trees. Descend quickly to cross Joe Wright Creek on a bridge. The trail then curves northwest with some views of Chambers Lake down and to your right. After 1.9 miles from the trailhead, cross Fall Creek on another bridge and pass a trail register and a Rawah Wilderness sign. After 3.1 more miles from the first Fall Creek crossing, you will have crossed the creek again and arrived at an overlook of Blue Lake down and to your right. Cameron Peak lies to the north northeast. This is the destination of this hike but the trail continues north northwest to a pass and down into more of the Rawah Wilderness. Blue Lake is a popular camping area. Hang Lake lies 0.2 miles above to the southwest and requires an easy bushwhack.

172

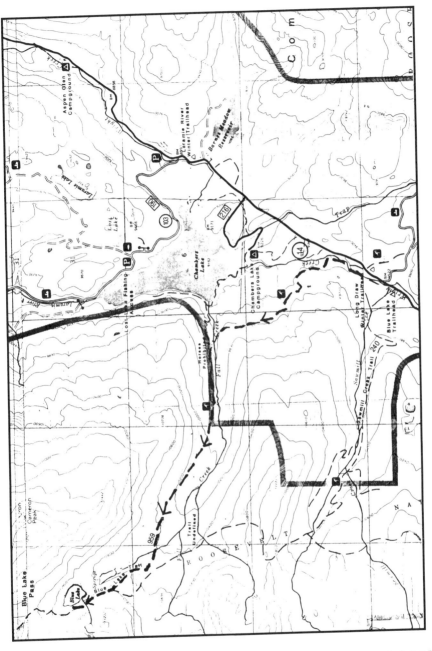

Courtesy of Trails Illustrated

41B Donner Pass and Lookout Mountain

Hike Distance: 2.9 miles each way
Hiking Time: Up in 85 minutes. Down in 65 minutes.
Starting Elevation: 8,840 feet
Highest Elevation: 10,626 feet (3,239 meters)
Elevation Gain: 1,906 feet (includes 60 feet extra each way)
Difficulty: Moderate
Steepness Index: 0.12
Trail: All but the last 0.2 miles
Relevant Maps: Crystal Mountain 7½ minute
Larimer County Number Four
Roosevelt National Forest
Views from the Summit: NW to West White Pine Mountain
S to Longs Peak
SW to Mummy Mountain
WSW to Signal Mountain

Getting There: Drive 6.7 miles west on U.S. 34 from its intersection with U.S. 287 in Loveland. Turn right and drive 5.2 miles north to Masonville. At Masonville take the left fork and continue on the main road for 10.7 miles to a fork and go left again. From this fork drive 10.2 miles up Buckhorn Canyon to a sign and the Ballard Road on your left. Drive up the Ballard Road for 2.9 miles to a trailhead sign on your left. Park in an open area on your right. On the Ballard Road take right forks at mile 0.1 and 0.3. Go straight at mile 1.0, right at mile 1.2 and left at mile 1.25. Regular cars can reach this trailhead.

The well-known Donner Pass in California was the site of a tragedy in the winter of 1847 when a group of immigrants were stranded and many died of starvation. This Donner Pass lacks such dramatic history but does lead to Lookout Mountain west of Loveland.

Begin the hike by crossing the road and going south past the trailhead sign and register. The trail rises and falls through a grove of aspen for a half mile to a fork and a sign. Go left at this important fork. The trail eventually merges with an old mining road and passes through a large area of old boards, remnants of an abandoned mine. After two miles from the trailhead you will reach a sign and a four-way intersection at Donner Pass. The trail to the right leads to Signal Mountain in 5 miles. Straight ahead descends to the Miller Fork and the Dunraven Trailhead. You take the left fork and ascend to the east northeast. In 0.15 miles the trail arrives at a fork and a sign. Go left (north) toward Lookout Mountain. In 0.4 miles farther the trail brings you to a saddle and several medium sized cairns in a clearing. Continue west into the trees on a faint trail which soon disappears. Lookout Mountain's rocky summit will be visible to the west so pick your way toward it with some easy hand work necessary near the top. A small cairn marks the high point and there is full 360 degree visibility. The key part of the descent is to go east and regain the trail which you left for your final ascent.

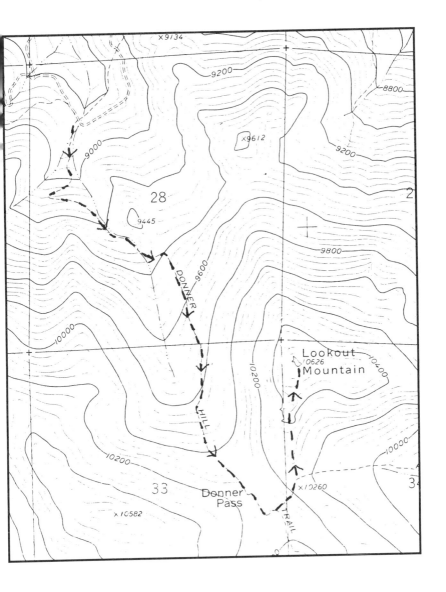

42A Shadow Mountain Lookout

Hike Distance:	5.1 miles each way
Hiking Time:	Up in 115 minutes. Down in 97 minutes.
Starting Elevation:	8,400 feet
Highest Elevation:	9,923 feet (3,025 meters)
Elevation Gain:	1,713 feet (includes an extra 95 feet each way)
Difficulty:	Moderate
Steepness Index:	0.06
Trail:	All the way
Relevant Maps:	Shadow Mountain 7½ minute
	Trails Illustrated Number 200

Grand County Number Two
Arapaho National Forest
Rocky Mountain National Park
Views from the Summit: N to Terra Tomah Mountain
NNW to Mount Richthofen and Grand Lake
NW to Bowen Mountain
E to Mount Craig
ESE to Mount Adams
SSW to Lake Granby
SE to Shadow Mountain
SW to Shadow Mountain Lake
WNW to Parkview Mountain

Getting There: From U.S. 40 west of Granby, drive north on U.S. 34 for 14.5 miles and turn right to enter Grand Lake Village. After 0.2 miles turn right onto Center Street. After 0.2 more miles turn left onto Marina Drive. After one block turn right onto Shadow Mountain Road. After 0.2 miles on this road turn right and cross a bridge. In another half mile turn left and in 150 yards farther, park on the right by the trailhead opposite a private home.

The hike to Shadow Mountain Lookout takes you along the eastern edge of Shadow Mountain Lake before ascending to the lookout tower. The vistas from the tower are very special so bring your camera. The lookout lies within Rocky Mountain National Park but no entrance fee is required for this trail.

Begin east on the Continental Divide Trail. After a half mile pass the boundary between the Arapaho National Forest and Rocky Mountain National Park. In 0.2 more miles pass a trailhead sign on your left. The trail continues along the side of Shadow Mountain Lake and in 0.8 more miles take a left fork and ascend to the east. The trail then reaches a ridge and follows it up to the lookout. No side trails are encountered. The stone and wooden observation tower can be ascended by stairs and offers wonderful views of the three lakes below and into Rocky Mountain National Park. You have no trail option for your return because you ascended on the only trail. There is no definite trail to the actual summit of Shadow Mountain which lies 0.6 miles east of the lookout tower.

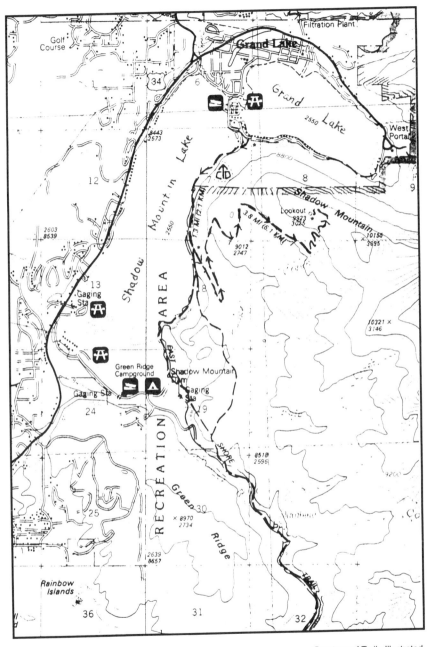

42B Beaver Lake

Hike Distance:	3.2 miles each way
Hiking Time:	Up in 96 minutes. Down in 83 minutes.
Starting Elevation:	8,280 feet
Highest Elevation:	9,746 feet (2,971 meters)
Elevation Gain:	1,546 feet (includes an extra 40 feet of elevation gain each way)
Difficulty:	Moderate
Steepness Index:	0.09
Trail:	All the way
Relevant Maps:	Grouse Mountain 7½ minute
	Trails Illustrated Number 121
	Eagle County Number Four
	White River National Forest

Getting There: From Interstate 70 take Exit 167 and drive south through Avon on Avon Road and up Village Road through Beaver Creek Village a total of 3.1 miles from I-70. There are several possible parking areas. One is just below the chapel on your left. Another is by the Service Center or the Fire House farther up the road. For this hike description consider your parking area to be the one below the chapel opposite The Inn at Beaver Creek.

Beaver Creek Village and the town of Avon have been expanding dramatically in the last few years. If you haven't seen this area lately, it is worth the trip. There are many large bronze sculptures, the golf course to the left of Village Road is magnificent and the large, palatial homes in Beaver Creek Village are striking.

From the parking area hike up Village Road past the chapel and turnoffs to the stables and to the fire station on your left. Continue up the paved Village Road to a turnaround area at the foot of some fine homes. Continue south past a "Private Road — Please Do Not Enter" sign which is intended for vehicles. In a hundred yards the paving ends. Continue around a metal barrier and signs prohibiting unauthorized vehicles. Follow this road upward to the south past a storage tank on your right and Beaver Creek on your left. Ascend through aspens. In 0.8 miles from the barrier, after passing under a chair lift, reach a T and turn left. Lose a little elevation over about 40 yards and then take a right fork and ascend south on a dirt road with Beaver Creek on your left. (A trail also ascends on the east side of Beaver Creek and can be accessed by continuing 200 feet farther past the right fork mentioned above and entering the trees and going south at several boulders and a red pole 300 yards south of a ski hut. Both trails will join about halfway up the valley.) In a hundred yards keep left at a fork and in another half mile avoid a right fork and cross Beaver Creek. Just past the creek crossing the trail along the east side of the creek joins your trail from the left. Continue up the valley over some more wooden walkways with the creek now on your right. In about 1.2 more miles you will reach serene, clear Beaver Lake. (The trail continues up and south past the lake to two higher lakes.) Enjoy the lake and return along Beaver Creek as you ascended.

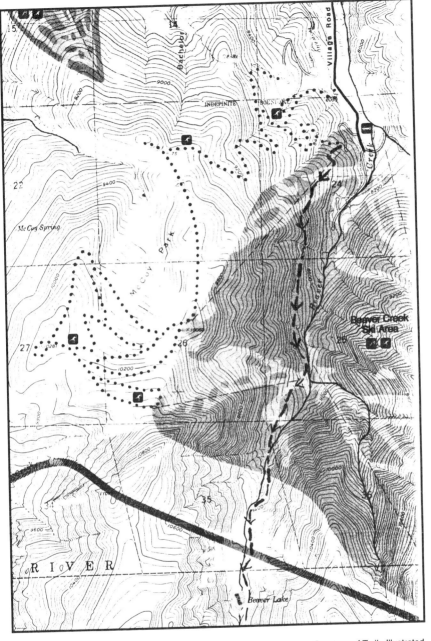

Courtesy of Trails Illustrated

179

43A Harvard Lakes

Hike Distance:	2.8 miles each way
Hiking Time:	Up in 83 minutes. Down in 70 minutes.
Starting Elevation:	9,440 feet
Highest Elevation:	10,340 feet (3,152 meters)
Elevation Gain:	1,050 feet (includes an extra 75 feet each way)
Difficulty:	Easy
Steepness Index:	0.07
Trail:	All the way
Relevant Maps:	Harvard Lakes 7½ minute
	Buena Vista West 7½ minute
	Trails Illustrated Number 129
	Chaffee County Number Two
	San Isabel National Forest
	Colorado Trail Map Number Twelve

Getting There: From the intersection of U.S. 24 and Colorado 300 in the center of Buena Vista, drive north on U.S. 24 for 0.4 miles and turn left onto Crossman Avenue which is Chaffee County Road 350. After 2.0 straight miles on this road you arrive at a T which is Chaffee Road 361. Go right for 0.9 miles and turn sharply left onto Chaffee Road 365. Follow the main dirt road for a total of 3.4 miles and park off the left side of the road. En route to this point, keep straight at mile 1.8 and go right at mile 2.3 and again at mile 3.1.

As winter approaches, the hiker should seek lower destinations in areas which normally experience less snowfall. This hike to the Harvard Lakes meets both criteria and utilizes a part of the Colorado Trail which was formerly called the Main Range Trail. Begin hiking at the trail signs on the north side of the road. The route initially is a bit steep and directly north before there is a switchback. The excellent trail continues generally north and west along the eastern flank of the foothills. Intially there are good views to the southwest up the North Cottonwood Creek drainage. In the middle third of the hike, the views are east toward the Arkansas Valley. Stay on the main trail and make two creek crossings before coming over a ledge to find Lower Harvard Lake on your right. A primitive trail circles this lake. A few minutes further up the main trail lies the Upper Harvard Lake on your left with the flanks of Mount Columbia, a fourteener, to the west. These two lakes are the terminus of this hike and provide beautiful settings for rest, reflection and refreshment before your return.

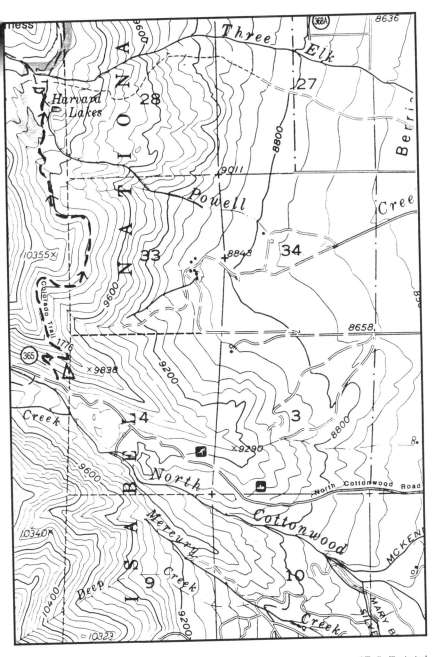

Courtesy of Trails Illustrated

43B Lost Lake (Boulder County)

Hike Distance:	1.8 miles each way
Hiking Time:	Up in 45 minutes. Down in 38 minutes.
Starting Elevation:	9,000 feet
Highest Elevation:	9,795 feet (2,985 meters)
Elevation Gain:	819 feet (includes 12 extra feet each way)
Difficulty:	Easy
Steepness Index:	0.09
Trail:	All the way
Relevant Maps:	Nederland 7½ minute
	Trails Illustrated Number 102
	Boulder County
	Roosevelt National Forest

Getting There: From the junction with Colorado 72 in Nederland, drive south on Colorado 119 for 0.6 miles and turn right (west). Keep right at 1.5 miles and drive 4.9 miles from Colorado 119 through the town of Eldora to a fork. Go left 0.2 miles farther and park at the former townsite of Hessie.

The easy hike to Lost Lake passes numerous cascades and waterfalls to reach a quiet lake with beautiful peaks to the west. Several connecting trails lead west to other lakes.

Begin hiking up the road to the west northwest from Hessie, an old mining town. In a quarter mile reach the Hessie Trailhead and the end of the four wheel drive road. Cross the North Fork of Boulder Creek and quickly reach a four-way intersection. Each of these three choices will eventually come together but go straight ahead and up through a partial clearing to reach a trail sign and a fork just before a brdige across a creek. The right fork leads to Jasper Lake and Devils Thumb Lake. You go left over the bridge and continue more steeply up to another fork and trail signs. Ascend to the left and reach Lost Lake in a steep half mile. A faint trail encircles the lake and above to the south lies Bryan Mountain and an abandoned mine building. Visible to the west are peaks along the Continental Divide.

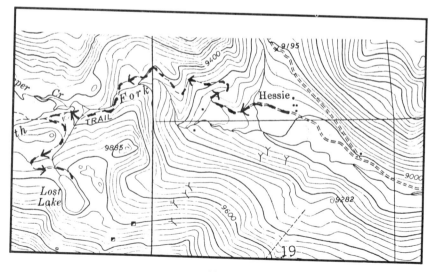

44A Holy Cross City

Hike Distance:	3.8 miles each way
Hiking Time:	Up in 128 minutes. Down in 93 minutes.
Starting Elevation:	9,320 feet
Highest Elevation:	11,408 feet (3,477 meters)
Elevation Gain:	2,142 feet (includes an extra 27 feet each way)
Difficulty:	Moderate
Steepness Index:	0.11
Trail:	All the way
Relevant Maps:	Mount of the Holy Cross 7½ minute
	Trails Illustrated Number 126
	Eagle County Number Four
	White River National Forest

Getting There: From Interstate 70 west of Vail, take U.S. 24 through Minturn for a total of 12.1 miles and turn right onto Homestake Road 703 which leads past the Blodgett Campground. Follow this excellent dirt road for 7.1 miles down the valley, paralleling Homestake Creek and park on the right side of the road at Gold Park near a sign about the four wheel drive road to Holy Cross City.

Here is a hike up a rough four wheel drive road to a ghost town. Holy Cross City flourished between 1880 and 1884. It provided housing for miners and their families and achieved a maximum population of about 300. Today extensive cabin ruins and many large metal mining implements are all that remain. There is a sense of peace in this grassy meadow with lovely vistas to the north and east.

From Gold Park, begin west up the rough road which winds through aspen groves with French Creek on the left. Occasional four wheelers and motorbikers may be encountered. In 1.5 miles a road joins your route from the left. Continue up to the northwest. In 1.4 more miles reach a wilderness signboard. Then cross French Creek and take a left fork at a wooden pole sign and continue more gradually to the southwest. In 0.9 miles from the signboard reach extensive mining ruins and the meadow above with the abandoned cabins and ruins of Holy Cross City. A footpath leads northwest into the heart of town. This pleasant spot makes a great picnic site. (One of the roads continues up and southwest about two miles to Fancy Pass.) Return by your ascent route.

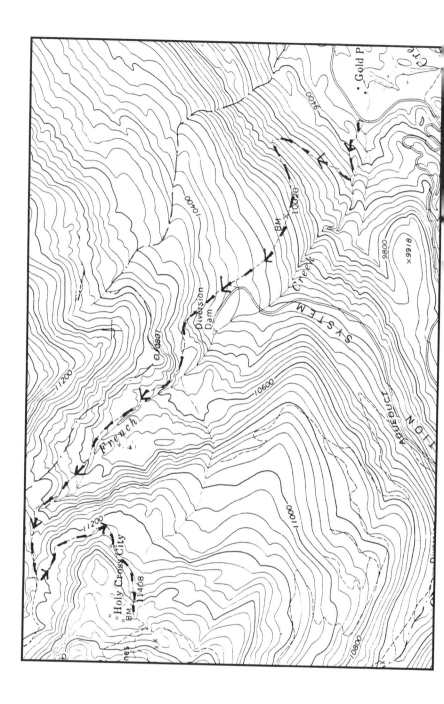

44B Gem Lake

Hike Distance:	2.0 miles each way
Hiking Time:	Up in 64 minutes. Down in 57 minutes.
Starting Elevation:	7,745 feet
Highest Elevation:	8,825 feet (2,690 meters)
Elevation Gain:	1,040 feet (includes an extra 30 feet of elevation gain each way)
Difficulty:	Easy
Steepness Index:	0.10
Trail:	All the way
Relevant Maps:	Estes Park 7½ minute
	Trails Illustrated Number 200
	Larimer County Number Four
	Rocky Mountain National Park

Getting There: From the junction of U.S. 34 and U.S. 36 in Estes Park, drive northwest on U.S. 34 for 0.4 miles and then turn right onto MacGregor Avenue which becomes the Devils Gulch Road. In 1.6 more miles past the turnoff onto MacGregor Avenue, park in the designated area off the left (north) side of the road.

The Estes Park area usually has a mild winter and Gem Lake can be reached in late fall. This hike lies mostly in Rocky Mountain National Park but no fee is required. Dogs are prohibited even on a leash. Beautiful rock formations are present throughout. The trail is clear and well maintained and the views south to Estes Park, Longs Peak and many other mountains are excellent.

Begin hiking west southwest past a llama enclosure on your left. (These are being introduced into the Rockies as pack animals.) In 0.7 miles from the trailhead you actually enter Rocky Mountain National Park. After 100 yards take the right fork. (The left fork leads to The Twin Owls, a recognizable rock formation.) In 0.1 miles take a left fork and continue northeast. In 0.8 more miles you will pass a rock formation on your left called "Paul Bunyan's Boot." After 0.4 more miles you will have passed a toilet on your left and have arrived at Gem Lake with high rocks to the east and northeast. Through the trees to the south Twin Sisters Peaks are visible.

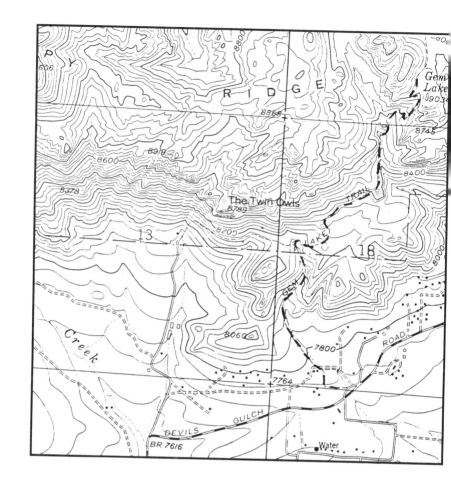

45A Crosier Mountain

Hike Distance:	4.3 miles each way
Hiking Time:	Up in 138 minutes. Down in 105 minutes.
Starting Elevation:	6,420 feet
Highest Elevation:	9,250 feet (2,819 meters)
Elevation Gain:	3,060 feet (includes an extra 115 feet each way)
Difficulty:	Moderate
Steepness Index:	0.13
Trail:	All the way
Relevant Maps:	Glen Haven 7½ minute
	Larimer County Number Four
	Roosevelt National Forest
Views from the Summit:	SW to Hallett Peak
	SSW to Twin Sisters Peaks, Mount Meeker and Longs Peak
	W to Mummy Range

Getting There: From U.S. 34 at Drake, take Road 43 (which parallels the North Fork of the Big Thompson River) toward Glen Haven for 2.2 miles and park in the designated area on the left at a gate and a trail sign.

Crosier Mountain lies in an area of relatively little snowfall and can usually be hiked without ice and snow problems between April and early December. This is one of three trails to the top of Crosier Mountain.

Begin your hike by going through the gate and turning west on the clear trail which quickly passes a larger trail sign and ascends steeply in a clearing before turning south into the trees. Another clearing is reached about 1.2 miles from the trailhead. After reaching a ridge, descend almost 100 feet into a ravine before ascending again and reaching a sparsely treed area with Crosier Mountain finally visible ahead to the west. Soon reach a fork and a trail sign. Take the left fork which ascends southwest for a half mile to the rocky, unmarked summit of Crosier Mountain. The views to the south and west are excellent, especially toward the "diamond" of the east face of Longs Peak. Return by trail as you ascended. (A less strenuous route up Crosier Mountain begins southeast from the town of Glen Haven and meets this route at the final trail intersection and sign.)

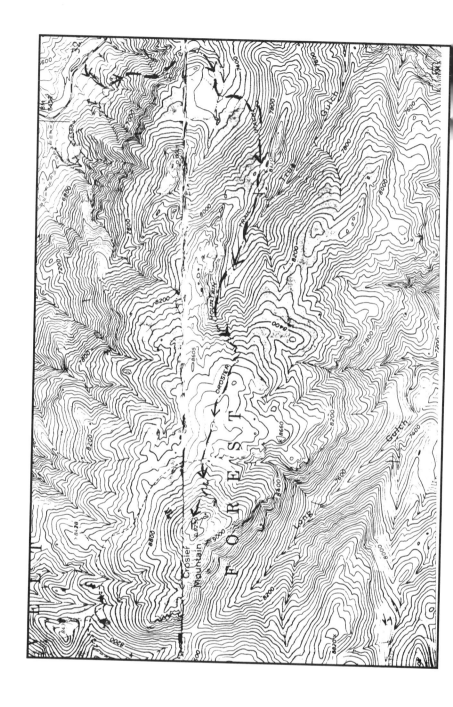

45B Sandbeach Lake

Hike Distance:	4.4 miles each way
Hiking Time:	Up in 115 minutes. Down in 95 minutes.
Starting Elevation:	8,380 feet
Highest Elevation:	10,283 feet (3,134 meters)
Elevation Gain:	2,303 feet (includes an extra 200 feet of elevation gain each way due to undulations in the trail)
Difficulty:	Moderate
Steepness Index:	0.10
Trail:	All the way
Relevant Maps:	Allens Park 7½ minute
	Trails Illustrated Number 200
	Boulder County
	Rocky Mountain National Park
	Roosevelt National Forest

Getting There: From the junction of U.S. 36 and Colorado 7 at the west end of Lyons, drive southwest on Colorado 7 for 21.2 miles and turn left at the sign to the Wild Basin Ranger Station. Continue for 0.4 miles on the paved road and turn right onto a dirt road. The Sandbeach Lake Trailhead and parking area are immediately on your right.

Located within Rocky Mountain National Park, the hike to Sandbeach Lake requires no park fee and pets are forbidden. For a lake hike, the elevation gain is substantial and the trail is up to the excellent standards of the National Park.

Begin north from the trailhead sign and follow the intermittently steep trail as it turns west. In 1.4 miles from the trailhead, keep left at a sign and fork. You will pass several cutoffs to campgrounds en route to a crossing of Campers Creek and then Hunters Creek until you finally reach the shores of Sandbeach Lake. Mount Orton lies to the west, Copeland Mountain to the southwest, Pagoda Peak to the northwest, and Longs Peak and Mount Meeker to the north northwest. Return as you ascended.

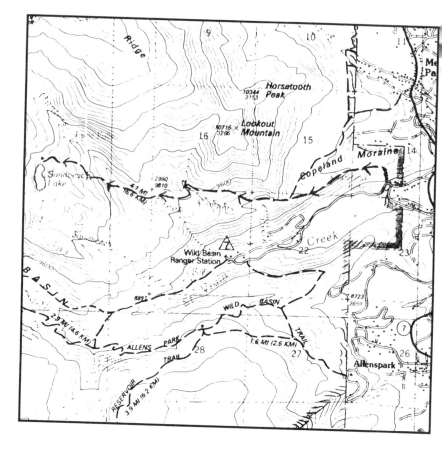

46A Colorado Trail: Kenosha Pass to Jefferson Creek

Hike Distance: 5.7 miles each way
Hiking Time: Out in 137 minutes. Back in 146 minutes.
Starting Elevation: 10,000 feet
Highest Elevation: 10,380 feet (3,164 meters)
Elevation Gain: 1,722 feet (includes many trail undulations)
Difficulty: Moderate
Steepness Index: 0.06
Trail: All the way
Relevant Maps: Jefferson 7½ minute
Park County Number One
Pike National Forest
Colorado Trail Map Number Five

Getting There: Drive on U.S. 285 to Kenosha Pass and park on the west side of the road at an open area near the entrance to the Kenosha Pass Campground. Kenosha Pass is 19 miles southwest of Bailey and 4 miles northeast of Jefferson.

Here is a hike which can be done from May into November. It uses the well-marked Colorado Trail as it proceeds west from Kenosha Pass to Jefferson Creek. (The Colorado Trail extends from Denver to Durango, a total of 469 meandering miles.)

Begin this hike by heading west into the Kenosha Pass Campground and taking two quick left forks and making a right turn off the road just after passing through an open fence. Signs facilitate these initial intersections. Cross two logging trails as you gradually ascend to reach a large area of dead trees and wonderful views of South Park and the mountains to the southwest in 1.2 miles from the trailhead. The trail rises and falls as it continues west across an old road before it crosses Guernsey Creek 2.5 miles from the trailhead. After passing two more dirt roads you will cross Deadman Creek in 1.9 miles from Guernsey Creek. Cairns will indicate part of the route as you follow trail markers to the left at two forks, pass through an area of burnt trees, and then through a gate before reaching the next trailhead at the public road just east of Jefferson Creek. (This point can be reached by passenger cars by way of Jefferson.) This is the destination of this hike. (The Colorado Trail will continue up to Georgia Pass and beyond.) Return by retracing your route as it rises and falls back to Kenosha Pass.

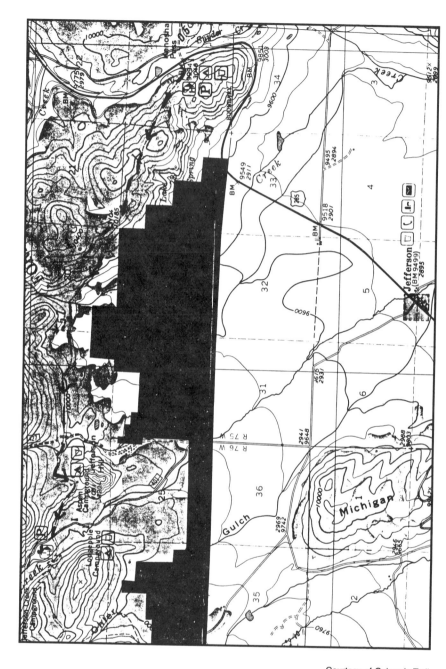

Courtesy of Colorado Trail

46B Panorama Point

Hike Distance:	3.7 miles each way
Hiking Time:	Up in 88 minutes. Down in 85 minutes.
Starting Elevation:	8,500 feet
Highest Elevation:	9,320 feet (2,841 meters)
Elevation Gain:	1,380 feet (includes 280 feet extra each way)
Difficulty:	Moderate
Steepness Index:	0.07
Trail:	All the way
Relevant Maps:	Black Hawk 7½ minute
	Tungsten 7½ minute
	Gilpin County
	Golden Gate Canyon State Park
Views from the Summit:	N to Twin Sisters Peaks
	NNE to Starr Peak
	NNW to Mount Audubon, Longs Peak and Mount Meeker
	NW to Devils Thumb, South Arapaho Peak and North Arapaho Peak
	SSW to Mount Evans
	SW to Grays Peak, Torreys Peak, Mount Eva, Mount Bancroft, Parry Peak and James Peak
	W to Thorn Lake

Getting There: Drive to Golden Gate Canyon State Park by either going west from Washington Street in Golden via Jefferson County Road 70 and Colorado 46 for 14.1 miles, or north from U.S. 6 on Colorado 119 and then east on Colorado 46. After entering the park, drive northwest on Mountain Base Road for 0.9 miles and park on an off road area on your left.

Golden Gate Canyon State Park is less than an hour by car from Denver. The park is excellent for families, requires a daily fee and contains many trails, picnic areas, campsites and other attractions. Fishing and horseback riding are permitted. The best overlook in the park is from Panorama Point.

The great view of the Indian Peaks and Longs Peak from Panorama Point and the Ken R. Larkin Memorial Shelter is assisted on a wooden deck by a plaque which names the peaks on the horizon. Ken was a young outdoorsman from Kansas City who loved the Colorado Mountains.

Start hiking north alongside the road for about 100 yards and then turn left onto the Elk Trail which winds northward up the valley. After 0.4 miles from the trailhead take a left fork and pass two cabin ruins on your left. In 1.8 more miles cross the paved Gap Road and continue to follow the symbols for the Elk Trail. Descend to a four-way intersection which is reached in 0.6 miles from the road. Then turn right onto the Raccoon Trail, cross the creek and ascend more steeply to the southeast and the wooden platforms of Panorama Point. The views from here are extraordinary.

The Ken R. Larkin Memorial panorama map will point out the mountains and passes which are visible from two separate vantage points. Panorama Point is also accessible by automobile. The viewing platform is wheelchair accessible and there are picnic tables and toilet facilities nearby.

Return as you ascended by the Raccoon and Elk Trails.

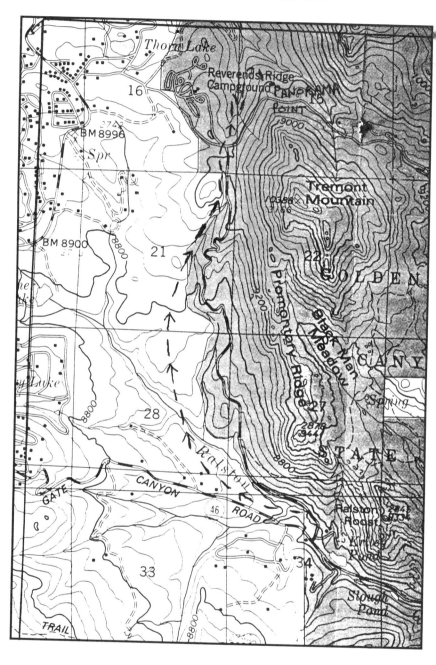

47A Mount Falcon

Hike Distance: 4.0 miles each way
Hiking Time: Up in 100 minutes. Down in 75 minutes.
Starting Elevation: 6,020 feet
Highest Elevation: 7,851 feet (2,393 meters)
Elevation Gain: 1,951 feet (includes 60 extra feet each way)
Difficulty: Moderate
Steepness Index: 0.09
Trail: All the way
Relevant Maps: Morrison 7½ minute
                     Jefferson County Number One
                     Mount Falcon Park (Jefferson County Open Space)
Views from the Summit: NNE to Mount Morrison
                       NNW to Longs Peak and Mount Meeker
                       NE to Red Rocks Park, Dakota Ridge and Green
                       Mountain
                       NW to Squaw Mountain and James Peak
                       ENE to Downtown Denver
                       SW to Rosalie Peak
                       WNW to Chief Mountain
                       WSW to Mount Evans

Getting There: Drive on Colorado 8, either 1.4 miles north from U.S. 285 or south from U.S. 74 in Morrison for 0.9 miles and turn west onto Forest Avenue. After 0.1 mile on Forest Avenue, turn right onto Vine Street and follow it for 0.3 miles to the end of the road at a large trailhead parking area.

This route up to Mount Falcon from the northeast is much more demanding than the approach from the west but the trailhead is less than 25 miles from downtown Denver. Due to its low elevation this hike can be made from April into November. The ruins of the Walker home and the site of a proposed summer White House are interesting side trips on the way to the summit. Mount Falcon Park is part of the Jefferson County Open Space. Dogs must be kept on a leash and motorized vehicles are forbidden on the trails.

Start your hike from a sign board at the northwest corner of the parking area. Proceed west southwest and stay on the Castle Trail. The trail passes some homes on your left before ascending west in a series of long switchbacks. Just before arriving at a fork on a ridge 2.4 miles from the trailhead, there is a shelter with a picnic bench on your right. Go left at the fork and stay on the Castle Trail. (The right fork takes you to "Walkers Dream," where John Brisben Walker tried to build and promote a summer residence for the President of the United States.) After 0.3 more miles on the Castle Trail you arrive at a four-way intersection. You go left on the Meadow Trail. (On the right are the ruins of the large Walker home, known as The Castle.) Descend some on the Meadow Trail before ascending to a fork. Proceed to the right and stay on the Meadow Trail. Quickly arrive at a four-way intersection and continue straight to reach the Tower Trail. Ascend now to the southwest, take a right fork near the top and soon arrive at the one story wooden lookout tower which marks the summit of Mount Falcon. Enjoy the view from the tower and some refreshment and reflection before exploring the park further or retracing your ascent route back to the trailhead.

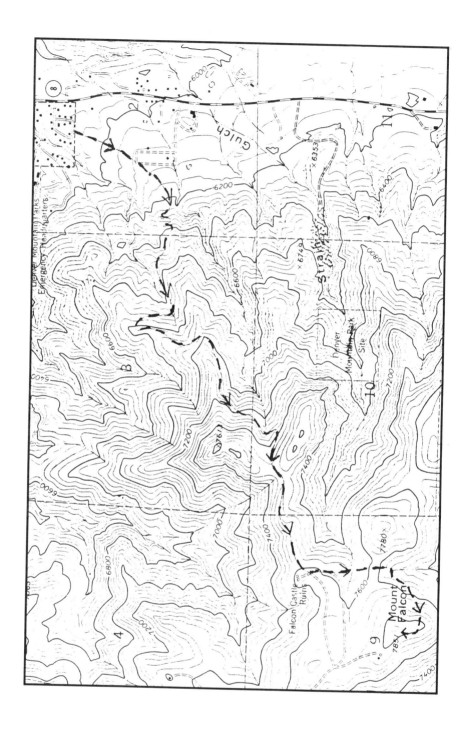

47B Sheep Mountain (Larimer County)

Hike Distance: 4.7 miles each way
Hiking Time: Up in 158 minutes. Down in 110 minutes.
Starting Elevation: 5,760 feet
Highest Elevation: 8,450 feet (2,576 meters)
Elevation Gain: 3,190 feet (includes 250 extra feet each way)
Difficulty: Moderate
Steepness Index: 0.13
Trail: All the way
Relevant Maps: Drake 7½ minute
                     Larimer County Number Four
                     Roosevelt National Forest
Views from the Summit: NW to Ypsilon Mountain
                     SSW to Mount Audubon and Mount Toll
                     SW to Mount Meeker and Longs Peak

Getting There: From the intersection with U.S. 287 in the middle of Loveland, drive west on U.S. 34 up through the Big Thompson Canyon for 13.2 miles to a dirt road on the left and a sign for the Round Mountain Recreation Area. Drive up this road for 0.2 miles to a parking area, restrooms and a trail sign. Park here.

Studying the names of Colorado's mountains is fascinating. Many commemorate historical people and places. Some are named for their configuration. Others are still unnamed awaiting the will of future Coloradans. Certain names have been given to several mountains in this state. Examples are Green, Bald, Ptarmigan and the hike for this week, Sheep Mountain.

The route to the top is the Round Mountain National Recreational Trail. (This peak presents a rounded summit from Loveland.) The trail is very clear, has informational signs about the ecology along the way and should be hikeable at least from April into November.

The hike begins northwest from the parking area up a blocked road past a trail register. This route is also called the Summit Adventure Trail on the trailhead map. Within five minutes, take a fork to the left and pass south over a large water pipe. The trail then curves east and continues on a shelf overlooking the Big Thompson Canyon. At several points, the trail descends before climbing again. Eventually you pass through some striking rock formations and then you reach a small spring about 3.1 miles from the trailhead. This is the only running water encountered along the entire hike.

Continue south southeast from the spring and lose some more elevation as the trail curves southwest up to a saddle. Then head west by trail past an overlook of Pine Reservoir to the south southeast. Cairns mark the trail near the top. A large cairn on a flat area and a nearby U.S.G.S. marker indicate the summit. Retrace your ascent route for the return.

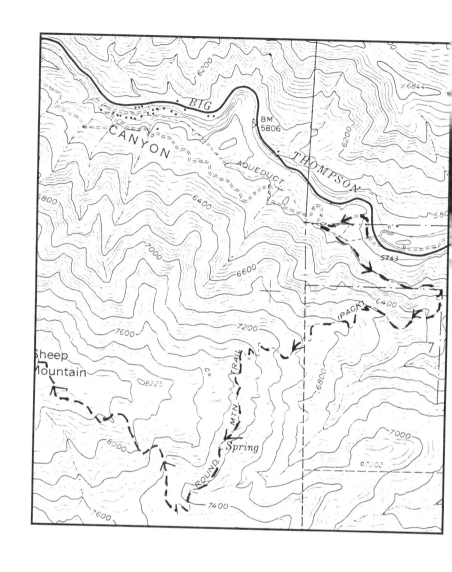

48A Hanging Lake

Hike Distance:	1.4 miles each way
Hiking Time:	Up in 38 minutes. Down in 26 minutes.
Starting Elevation:	6,120 feet
Highest Elevation:	7,170 feet (2,185 meters)
Elevation Gain:	1,070 feet (includes an extra 10 feet each way)
Difficulty:	Easy
Steepness Index:	0.15
Trail:	All the way
Relevant Maps:	Trails Illustrated Number 123
	Shoshone 7½ minute
	Garfield County Number Five
	White River National Forest

Getting There: Drive to the Hanging Lake Trailhead at mile 125.7 of Interstate 70 on the north side of the Colorado River near the eastern portal of the Hanging Lake Tunnel. (This point is 9.7 miles east of Glenwood Springs at Exit 116.) Park off the road to the north at a large designated area.

Here is a popular, easy hike to a very scenic and unusual lake. Due to its low elevation, Hanging Lake makes an especially attractive late or early season hike. There are several benches along the trail and picnic tables at the trailhead. Dogs are forbidden.

Begin hking to the north from a trail sign. The rocky trail ascends the canyon and crosses a number of bridges as you rise through the trees. Some flowing water is encountered in the final third of the route. Just before the lake the trail turns north and ascends a rocky shelf with metal railings for security. Then, before Hanging Lake the Spouting Rock Trail ascends up to the left and a boardwalk to the right takes you along the southern edge of the green bottomed lake which is fed from above by Spouting Rock.

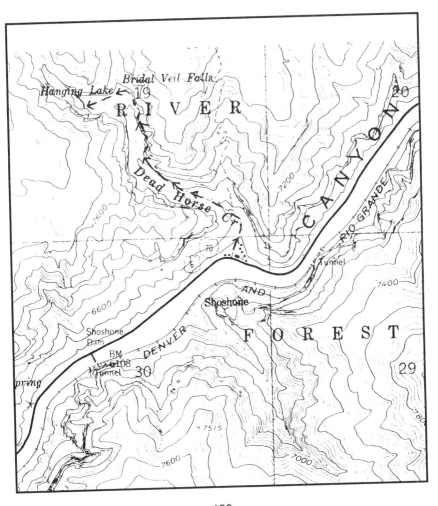

48B Chautauqua Park to the Amphitheater

Hike Distance:	Up in 1.7 miles. Down in 1.6 miles. (loop)
Hiking Time:	Up in 53 minutes. Down in 40 minutes.
Starting Elevation:	5,670 feet
Highest Elevation:	6,280 feet (1,914 meters)
Elevation Gain:	1,100 feet (includes an extra 490 feet due to undulations in the trail)
Difficulty:	Easy
Steepness Index:	0.12
Trail:	All the way
Relevant Maps:	Eldorado Springs 7½ minute
	Boulder Mountain Park Trail Map
	Boulder County

Getting There: From Broadway in Boulder, drive 1.1 miles southwest up Baseline Road and turn left onto a parking area at Chautauqua Park.

Boulder has many fine hiking trails close to town. This one, which begins at historic Chautauqua Park, ascends grassy slopes and then enters the forest. It offers good views of Boulder to the east and the flatirons to the west. There are many gains and losses of elevation on this route.

From the parking area, cross the road to the west and ascend the Chautauqua Trail which rises steeply into the trees and ends after 0.6 miles at a sign and T. Go right on the Baird-Bluebell Trail and keep right and then left at the next two forks and then straight at a four-way trail intersection. Then after taking a left fork and descending into Gregory Canyon, join the Amphitheater Trail just before a bridge crossing to a parking area. You will reach this point in 1.2 miles. Ascend the Amphitheater Trail which proceeds steeply southeast. Keep left at two forks and arrive at a rocky area, known as the Amphitheater, just before the trail joins the Saddle Rock Trail. The Amphitheater is a good spot for a break. For variety, return on the Saddle Rock Trail which descends southwest from a trail sign. After 17 minutes on the trail, keep straight at a fork and a minute later reach a parking area and toilets. Pick up the Baird-Bluebell Trail to your right and cross the bridge to retrace your way back to the trailhead at Chautauqua Park.

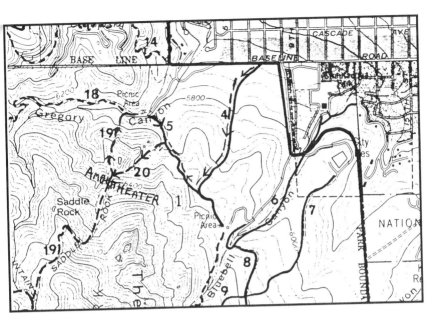

49A Deer Creek

Tour Distance:	2.3 miles each way
Tour Time:	Up in 80 minutes. Down in 42 minutes.
Starting Elevation:	10,550 feet
Highest Elevation:	11,400 feet (3,475 meters)
Elevation Gain:	880 feet (includes an extra 15 feet each way)
Avalanche Danger:	Least
Difficulty:	More Difficult
Steepness Index:	0.07
Trail:	All the way
Relevant Maps:	Montezuma 7½ minute
	Trails Illustrated Number 104
	Trails Illustrated Cross-Country Skier's Map Number 401
	Summit County Number Two
	Arapaho National Forest (Dillon Ranger District)

Getting There: From Exit 205 from Interstate 70, drive east on U.S. 6 for 7.7 miles and turn right into the Keystone Ski Area. Take the first left turn. (This is the Montezuma Road which bypasses the Keystone Ski Area.) Follow this road for 7.0 miles from U.S. 6 up through Montezuma to road end and park in an open area. (En route to this point take the right fork at 0.4 miles, at 4.8 miles and again at 6.7 miles from U.S. 6.)

Here is a ski tour which provides some steeper areas in a beautiful basin. The road to the parking area is maintained by Summit County and it should be reachable by regular cars. Several other ski tours originate in this area.

Begin south from the parking area and ascend moderately, keeping Deer Creek on your left. After 9 minutes, fork to the left and keep low in the valley. Continuing to the south you will pass through a fence at a National Forest sign and 17 minutes later the trail descends slightly to the left and easily crosses the creek. The ascent through the trees, on the left side of the valley

201

with Deer Creek on your right, now becomes steeper. This tour description ends at a point about 150 feet below timberline when the trail levels out at a trail fork with the open valley nearby on your right and rocky Radical Hill visible above to your left (east). If you want to proceed farther, continue southwest and south up into the basin or return as you ascended. You will probably need to do some side-stepping on the steeper, higher areas of the descent.

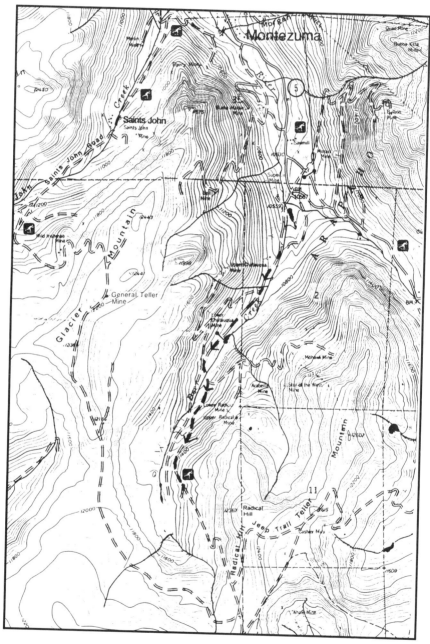

Courtesy of Trails Illustrated

49B Chinns Lake

Tour Distance: 3.7 miles each way
Tour Time: Up in 130 minutes. Down in 50 minutes.
Starting Elevation: 9,560 feet
Highest Elevation: 11,040 feet (3,365 meters)
Elevation Gain: 1,580 feet (includes 50 extra feet each way)
Avalanche Danger: Moderate
Difficulty: More Difficult
Steepness Index: 0.08
Trail: All the way
Relevant Maps: Empire 7½ minute
                     Trails Illustrated Number 103
                     Clear Creek County
                     Arapaho National Forest

Getting There: Drive 2.0 miles west of Idaho Springs on Interstate 70 and take Exit 238. After 0.3 miles go right and ascend Fall River Road for 6.8 miles. Park off the road as it curves to the right and there is a side road on the left.

The trailhead to Chinns Lake lies within one hour of Denver and the route is rarely crowded. The last 1.5 miles are quite steep and will require good snow conditions in order to be enjoyable.

Start your skiing to the west from the road and cross Fall River. Soon you pass a cabin and after 0.6 miles from the trailhead you will cross the river again. As you ascend the valley to the west, stay on the wide main road and take first a left and later a right fork before another crossing of Fall River. Pass some old mine remnants. After 2.2 miles from the trailhead you reach a fork. The left fork ascends steeply to the west southwest and will be your route to Chinns Lake. The right fork leads through two gate posts and reaches Fall River Reservoir in another mile.

Continue up the left fork and be prepared for considerable herringbone skiing or side-stepping as you rise steeply for another mile and a half to the lake. The road bends sharply to the left just before you reach the open flat area at Chinns Lake. An old cabin is located along the lake. Witter Peak looms above to the west southwest. Mount Eva lies to the west northwest and Mount Bancroft to the north northwest. The setting is very scenic. Enjoy it before your rapid descent.

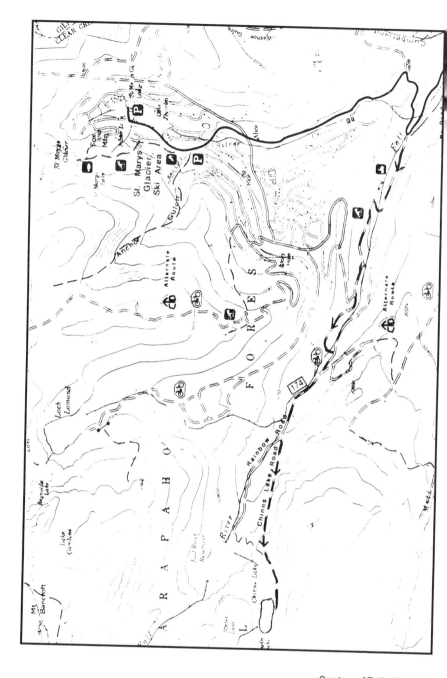

Courtesy of Trails Illustrated

204

50A Old Railroad Run

Tour Distance:	2.5 miles each way
Tour Time:	Out in 50 minutes. Back in 60 minutes.
Starting Elevation:	10,424 feet
Highest Elevation:	10,424 feet (Tennessee Pass) (3,177 meters)
Elevation Gain:	334 feet (includes an extra 5 feet each way)
Avalanche Danger:	Least
Difficulty:	Easiest
Steepness Index:	0.03
Trail:	All the way
Relevant Maps:	Leadville 7½ minute
	Pando 7½ minute
	Trails Illustrated Number 109
	Trails Illustrated Cross-Country Skier's Map Number 403
	Eagle County Number Four
	White River National Forest

Getting There: From the junction of Colorado 91 and U.S. 24 north of Leadville, drive northwest on U.S. 24 for 8.9 miles to Tennessee Pass and park in the designated area on the left at the pass (opposite the road to Ski Cooper).

This tour utilizes a segment of the Colorado Trail and an old railroad bed. Therefore the grade is very gentle. The adjacent downhill slopes of Ski Cooper make this a good outing for families or groups with both downhill and cross-country skiers.

Begin west northwest from the Colorado Trail sign on the west side of Tennessee Pass. In 0.4 miles keep right as you pass a kiln remnant on the left. Colorado Trail signs will appear at intervals. In 2.1 miles from the trailhead the Colorado Trail forks to the right and leaves the railroad bed. You keep left on the railroad bed and in 0.4 more miles arrive at the end point of this tour at a Mitchell Loop trail sign on a tree to the left with an open valley to your right. Galena Mountain and Homestake Peak are visible to the west southwest. Ascend back to Tennessee Pass by retracing your path. As you approach the pass, the ski slopes on Cooper Hill will be straight ahead.

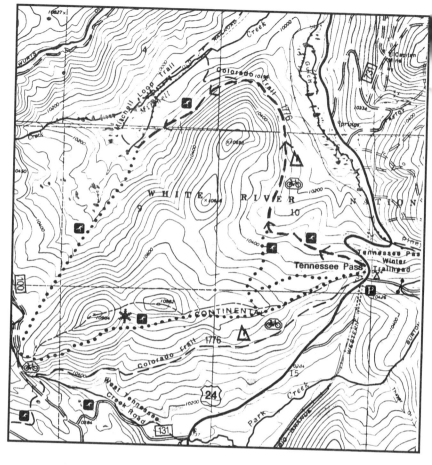

Courtesy of Trails Illustrated

50B No Name Gulch

Tour Distance:	3.9 miles each way
Tour Time:	Up in 100 minutes. Down in 52 minutes.
Starting Elevation:	9,190 feet
Highest Elevation:	10,560 feet (3,219 meters)
Elevation Gain:	1,370 feet
Avalanche Danger:	Least
Difficulty:	Easiest
Steepness Index:	0.07
Trail:	All the way
Relevant Maps:	Pando 7½ minute
	Trails Illustrated Number 109
	Trails Illustrated Cross-Country Skier's Map Number 403
	Eagle County Number Four
	White River National Forest

Getting There: From Exit 171 off Interstate 70 (west of Vail), drive south on U.S. 24 for 13.9 miles to an unplowed road on the right and a stop sign. This is the No Name Road. Park somewhere nearby, off U.S. 24. There is a side road on the left about 300 yards farther south with space to park. (The No Name Road is 0.8 miles north of the bridge over the railroad tracks on U.S. 24.)

The tour up the No Name Gulch Road is excellent for the beginning nordic skier. The road is quite gradual and the grade is constantly upward with no loss of elevation between the trailhead and the end point of this tour. The road experiences a low volume of cross-country traffic since it is somewhat isolated.

Begin southwest from the west side of U.S. 24 and follow the main road at all times as it slowly ascends through the trees via several switchbacks to the southwest. There are no particular landmarks along the way. The destination of this tour is reached when the road begins its first descent and Homestake Peak can be seen to the south southwest. The road continues for about four more miles south toward the Continental Divide if you wish for a longer ski tour. The return is a wonderful and gentle, totally downhill run back to U.S. 24.

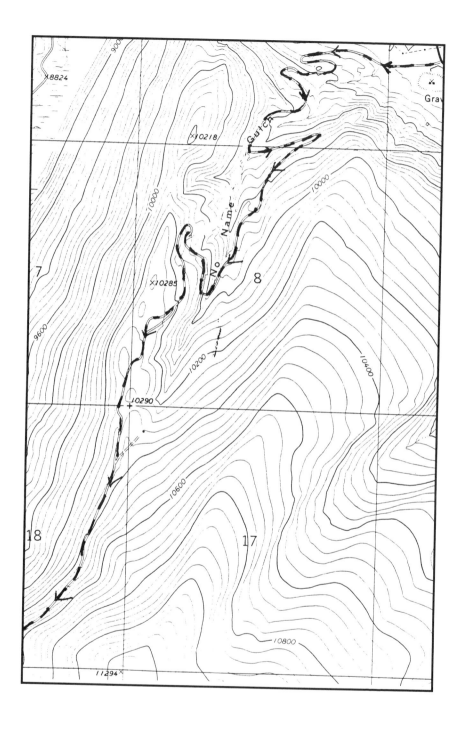

51A Jones Pass Road

Tour Distance:	2.4 miles each way
Tour Time:	Up in 92 minutes. Down in 50 minutes.
Starting Elevation:	10,440 feet
Highest Elevation:	12,000 feet (3,658 meters)
Elevation Gain:	1,610 feet (includes an extra 25 feet of elevation gain each way)
Avalanche Danger:	Significant
Difficulty:	More Difficult
Steepness Index:	0.13
Trail:	All the way
Relevant Maps:	Berthoud Pass 7½ minute
	Byers Peak 7½ minute
	Trails Illustrated Number 103
	Clear Creek County
	Arapaho National Forest

Getting There: From the stop light in Empire, drive west on U.S. 40 for 7.35 miles and turn off left on the road to the Henderson Mine at the sharp bend in the road. Keep right at 0.5 miles and again at 1.8 miles from U.S. 40. In 0.6 more miles park on your left. The Henderson Mine will be farther to your left.

The Jones Pass Road tour involves a considerable elevation gain and likely contact with snowmobiles. The road over Jones Pass can be negotiated by four wheel drive vehicles in the summer but dead ends in the valley below to the west.

Begin north northwest and up the Jones Pass four wheel drive road from the parking area. Within 0.2 miles take the right fork and ascend more steeply. After another half mile you will reach a clearing. Take a left fork, lose a little elevation and continue on the road which soon will curve to the south. In 1.7 more miles you will reach timberline and a large basin with many gradual areas for unrestricted ski touring. This tour description ends at 12,000 feet but if the snow on the road is suitable, you may wish to continue more steeply upward to Jones Pass at 12,451 feet. The return provides many open, rapidly descending runs. Beware of avalanche dangers above timberline.

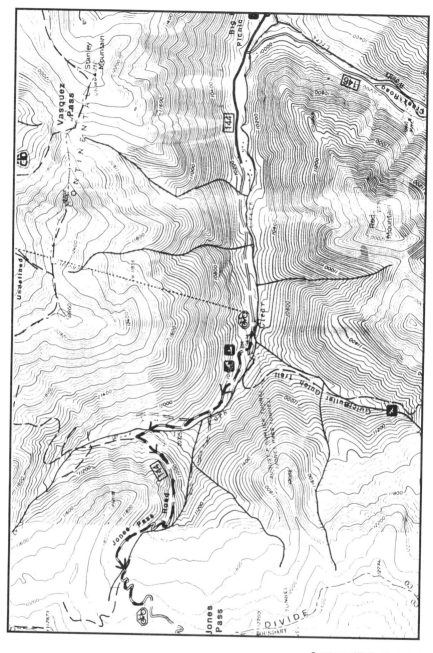

Courtesy of Trails Illustrated

51B Mesa Cortina Trail

Tour Distance:	4.8 miles each way
Tour Time:	Out in 94 minutes. Back in 85 minutes.
Starting Elevation:	9,220 feet
Highest Elevation:	9,700 feet (2,957 meters)
Elevation Gain:	830 feet (includes an extra 175 feet each way)
Avalanche Danger:	Least
Difficulty:	More Difficult
Steepness Index:	0.03
Trail:	All the way
Relevant Maps:	Dillon 7½ minute
	Frisco 7½ minute
	Willow Lakes 7½ minute
	Trails Illustrated Number 108
	Trails Illustrated Cross-Country Skier's Map Number 401
	Summit County Number Two
	Arapaho National Forest (Dillon Ranger District)

Getting There: Drive north on Colorado 9 from I-70 (Exit 205) in Silverthorne for 300 yards and turn left onto Wildernest Road. After 0.2 miles from Colorado 9 take the right fork and a quick left onto Buffalo Mountain Drive. After 1.0 mile from Colorado 9, turn right onto Lakeview Drive and after 0.4 miles farther take the left fork up Aspen Drive and after 0.15 miles more park on your left. The trailhead sign is on the right side of the road at this point.

The Mesa Cortina Trail enters the Gore Range Wilderness and leads into the South Willow Creek Trail. This route is very popular and proceeds through the woods mostly on footpaths. There are good views down to Silverthorne from the early part of the trail and Buffalo Mountain can be seen to the southwest in the final stages of the tour. The trail rises and dips a great deal and there are a few steep parts. Pets must be kept on a leash.

Start the tour by skiing west from the trailhead sign. Keep right (north) at a fork in a clearing which is reached in just a few minutes from the trailhead. In about 1.2 miles from the trailhead pass wilderness signs and ascend more steeply to the southwest. After 1.3 miles take another right fork leading to the northwest. Soon you will pass a trail sign and 0.3 miles later you will cross South Willow Creek and reach a junction with the Gore Range Trail. Take the left fork and gently ascend the valley to the southwest. In 100 yards past the Gore Range Trail take another right fork and continue to the west. Cross some open, level areas and then ascend more steeply into the trees to reach trail signs for the Buffalo Mountain Trail leading south and the South Willow Creek Trail which has brought you to this point. This is the destination for this tour. The open meadow just below is actually a better turn around point. Save some energy for the return since much of it is uphill.

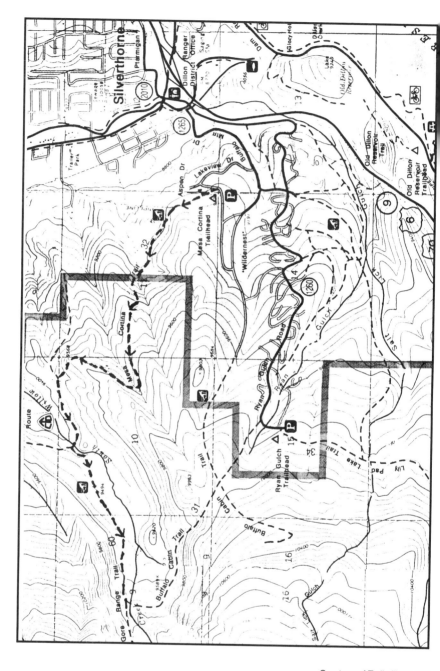

Courtesy of Trails Illustrated

52A Montezuma to Webster Pass

Tour Distance:	3.7 miles each way
Tour Time:	Up in 160 minutes. Down in 84 minutes.
Starting Elevation:	10,530 feet
Highest Elevation:	12,096 feet (Webster Pass) (3,687 meters)
Elevation Gain:	1,666 feet (includes an extra 50 feet each way)
Avalanche Danger:	Significant
Difficulty:	More Difficult
Steepness Index:	0.08
Trail:	All the way
Relevant Maps:	Montezuma 7½ minute
	Trails Illustrated Number 104
	Trails Illustrated Cross-Country Skier's Map Number 401
	Summit County Number Two
	Arapaho National Forest (Dillon Ranger District)

Getting There: Leave Interstate 70 at Exit 205 and drive east on U.S. 6 for 7.7 miles and turn right into the Keystone Ski Area. Within 50 yards take the first left turn onto the Montezuma Road and follow this road for 6.8 miles and park off the road on the right just past a side road on the left.

Webster Pass connects the Snake River Valley and Montezuma on the west with the Hall Valley and U.S. 285 northeast of Kenosha Pass. Webster Pass is a four wheel drive road today but it was a toll road in the latter 1800s and was named after the two brothers who built it.

For ski touring this route provides a beautiful trip up the wide Snake River Valley surrounded by impressive peaks.

As you approach timberline, if the road becomes obscure, proceed toward the solitary sign which will be visible above at the pass. Two segments of fencing above timberline indicate where the road can be found. Be especially careful about the avalanche possibilities.

Begin your ski tour by ascending to the east up the wide road on your left just before where you parked. A wooden sign marks the beginning of this road. The road rises briskly one half mile to a fork and a sign. Keep right (east southeast) and in 0.7 miles farther pass a cabin ruin on your left and cross the Snake River. (With the old cabin, a large flat area and excellent vistas this could be an excellent, easier destination.) The road now gets steeper as you ascend the basin. The sign at Webster Pass can be seen. Pass a fork and keep left as the right fork crosses over to Deer Creek. Stay on the road if possible and reach Webster Pass at the signboard. Handcart Gulch lies ahead to the southeast with Handcart Peak to the southwest and Red Cone to the east southeast. The return can be exhilarating, especially if the snow conditions are good.

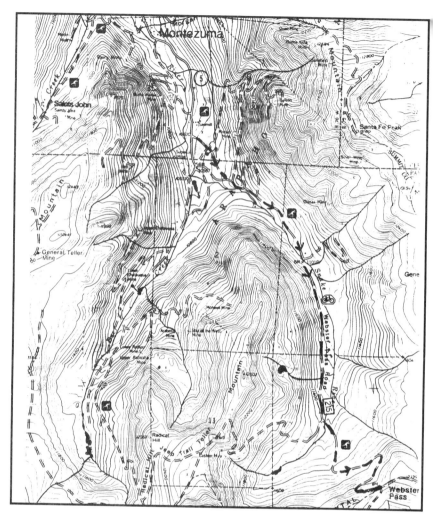

52B **Upper Michigan Ditch** ^{Courtesy of Trails Illustrated}

Tour Distance: 2.2 miles each way
Tour Time: Out in 50 minutes. Back in 49 minutes.
Starting Elevation: 10,276 feet (Cameron Pass)
Highest Elevation: 10,320 feet (3,146 meters)
Elevation Gain: 84 feet (includes an extra 25 feet each way)
Avalanche Danger: Least
Difficulty: Easiest
Steepness Index: 0.01
Trail: All the way
Relevant Maps: Clark Peak 7½ minute
    Chambers Lake 7½ minute
    Fall River Pass 7½ minute
    Trails Illustrated Number 200
    Trails Illustrated Number 112

Jackson County Number Four
Routt National Forest

Getting There: From U.S. 287 northwest of Fort Collins, drive west on Colorado 14 up Poudre Canyon for 57.8 miles to Cameron Pass and park in the designated area on the right (west) side of the road.

The drive from Fort Collins up Poudre Canyon to Cameron Pass is beautiful but lengthy. The lower areas don't receive a great deal of snow, but around Cameron Pass the snow pack should be adequate from December through March for ski touring.

The tour along the Upper Michigan Ditch follows a very level road along an aqueduct and provides dramatic views of the Nokhu Crags to the south southwest.

Begin your tour by crossing Colorado 14 to a stop sign on the east side of the road. Proceed southeast on a wide road into the woods. Follow the main road parallel to the drainage ditch past a few cabins and eventually curve to the south and reach a fork and some signs. The left fork leads more steeply to the American Lakes and the right fork continues on a level along the aqueduct to Lake Agnes. This fork is the destination of this tour. The easy glide back to Cameron Pass requires the same time as your outward trek. The Diamond Peaks may be visible to the northwest on your return.

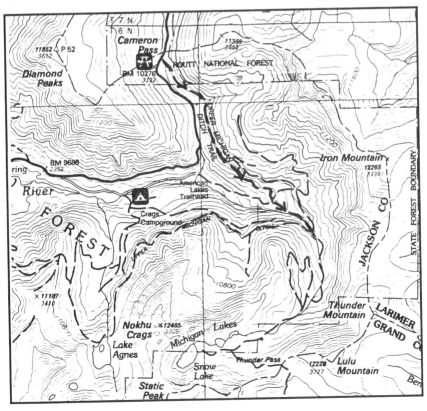

Courtesy of Trails Illustrated

REFERENCES

1. Boddie, Caryn and Boddie, Peter. *The Hikers Guide to Colorado*. Billings and Helena, Montana: Falcon Press Publishing Company Incorporated, 1984.
2. Borneman, Walter R. and Lampert, Lyndon, L. *A Climbing Guide to Colorado's Fourteeners*. Boulder, Colorado: Pruett Publishing Company, 1990.
3. Dannen, Kent and Dannen, Donna. *Rocky Mountain National Park Hiking Trails: Including Indian Peaks*. Chester, Connecticut: The Globe Pequot Press, 1989.
4. Gilliland, Mary Ellen. *The New Summit Hiker*. Silverthorne, Colorado: Alpenrose Press, 1992.
5. Gilliland, Mary Ellen. *The Vail Hiker*. Silverthorne, Colorado: Alpenrose Press, 1988.
6. Hagen, Mary. *Hiking Trails of Northern Colorado*. Boulder, Colorado: Pruett Publishing Company, 1987.
7. Jacobs, Randy. Editor. *Guide to the Colorado Mountains*. Denver, Colorado: Colorado Mountain Club, Ninth Edition, 1992.
8. Litz, Brian and Lankford, Kurt. *Skiing Colorado's Backcountry*. Golden, Colorado: Fulcrum, Inc., 1989.
9. Martin, Bob. *Hiking Trails of Central Colorado*. Boulder, Colorado: Pruett Publishing Company, 1989.
10. Roach, Gerry. *Colorado's Indian Peaks Wilderness Area: Classic Hikes and Climbs*. Golden, Colorado: Fulcrum, Inc., 1989.
11. Roach, Gerry. *Rocky Mountain National Park: Classic Hikes and Climbs*. Golden, Colorado: Fulcrum, Inc., 1988.
12. Roach, Gerry. *Colorado's Fourteeners*. Golden, Colorado: Fulcrum, Inc., 1992.

INDEX

INDEX

INDEX

INDEX

INDEX

INDEX

INDEX

INDEX